mrs. neal's not-so-conventional

MEDITATION
[CLASS] for TEENS

When the student is ready, the teacher will appear.

Nancy Neal

the meditation lady

BALBOA.
PRESS

A DIVISION OF HAY HOUSE

Scripture taken from the King James Version of the Bible.

Balboa Press books may be ordered through booksellers or by contacting:

Balboa Press
A Division of Hay House
1663 Liberty Drive
Bloomington, IN 47403
www.balboapress.com
1 (877) 407-4847

Print information available on the last page.

ISBN: 978-1-5043-3512-6 (sc)
ISBN: 978-1-5043-3513-3 (e)

Library of Congress Control Number: 2015909851

Balboa Press rev. date: 8/28/2015

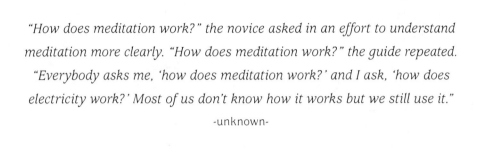

"How does meditation work?" the novice asked in an effort to understand meditation more clearly. "How does meditation work?" the guide repeated. "Everybody asks me, 'how does meditation work?' and I ask, 'how does electricity work?' Most of us don't know how it works but we still use it."

-unknown-

Let my teaching drop as the rain,
my speech distill as the dew,
as raindrops on the tender herb,
and as showers upon the grass.

– Deuteronomy 32:2

God sent a message to me many years ago.
He does that, doesn't He? He sends us messages.
Sometimes we hear them, sometimes we don't.

This one, I heard…

For He shall give his angels charge over thee,

to keep thee in all thy ways.

– Psalms 91:11

THE VISION

I have great memories of my youth, a large part of which was spent on a ranch in the Pacific Northwest in the 1960s.

A favorite memory of mine:

I used to ride my horse through the woods on the mountain behind our house. There were days when I would be out in those woods for hours — riding, exploring, and sometimes resting.

I would ride across the mountain up to a clearing in a meadow, get off of my horse and take off his bridle so he could graze, and I would lean up against one of my favorite trees, just sitting there pondering life. I could feel the warmth of the earth under my legs and the roughness of the tree trunk against my back. I would focus on the feeling of the sun on my face, the sounds and smells of the forest, and the scents from the trees, grasses, and wildflowers.

I didn't know it at the time, but I was meditating. I would sit in that clearing in those woods with my back against that tree, and *sense* everything around me.

I could feel the presence of God there.

In May of 1993, I found myself going through a phase of deep introspection. There was a lot going on in my life at that time.

I was at a crossroad trying to decide where I was going with my career, and trying to resolve some unresolved issues that were hanging around in my head from my younger years.

Sometimes it helps to take a moment to look back on your life to see more clearly where you need to move forward. I had been praying for months for a little guidance on where I was going; apparently, my prayers were heard.

A woman I knew — Jane, I will call her — intended to help me by guiding me through a meditation to assist with this going back to move forward thing. She had offered to lead me in meditation to a place where I could find my path.

It began simply enough with the relaxation techniques most of us use in meditation, but then it took an interesting turn.

Jane started a guided meditation to help bring me to a point where I could resolve a few issues I had with my mother who had passed away several years earlier.

Jane was trying to bring me to a beach. I could see a beach, and I could see my younger adult self on that beach. I love the ocean; I could feel myself moving toward the water.

Jane told me to pick up a stick and begin to write in the sand. She didn't tell me specifically what to write, just to write whatever was on my heart.

As I started to look for a stick, my even younger self began pulling me in a different direction. I realized I was in the woods.

Jane asked me if I wanted to read what I was writing in the sand, I told her there was no sand. She asked about the beach, and I said there was no beach.

I was in a forest.

From that point on, I was unaware of being in that room, and I could not hear Jane speaking to me.

I found myself on the ranch where I grew up, and I was on the mountain where I used to spend so much of my time. I was in my forest and I was a child again.

As I walked through the woods, I picked up some sticks and made some sort of sculpture with them. It was just a pile of sticks, but it resembled something vaguely familiar.

I smiled, and I continued on my walk.

I moved forward along that path where I had ridden my horse so many times, and I came to the clearing where I used to sit to ponder the meaning of life when I was a kid.

As I walked out into this clearing, I realized I had become an adult. There was a long, flowing fabric coming out from my waist like a huge skirt, and it was covering the ground in the clearing. It looked so soft and billowy.

Then I heard the laughter of children. I always have loved the laughter of children — it's my favorite sound.

As I looked around me, I could see hundreds of little children hiding behind the trees at the edge of the clearing. They were peeking out at me and giggling. I motioned to them to join me and they began to come out from behind the trees.

As they moved toward me, some were aging, but only to a teen age — no older than maybe 16 or 17. They came toward me and sat on that billowy fabric that had filled the clearing. Some moved closer to me and reached for my hands. I reached out to touch their hands.

I could feel my smile. I could feel joy.

And, I could feel a presence behind me; I knew it was my protector, my guardian. I knew I was safe.

Then I felt warmth from above me. I looked up and saw a great light. A huge ball of fire was moving slowly toward me from above, held by two large hands.

As it got closer, the hands and the ball of fire got smaller until they were floating before me.

The two hands hovered for a moment in front of me, holding this little ball of light. As it was placed into my hands, I heard the words — as clearly as if someone were standing there speaking to me — "Plant the seed of light."

Just as quickly as I had entered the forest, I was back in the room with Jane.

I sat up suddenly, silent.

She asked, "Are you all right?"

I nodded.

It seemed like hours had passed, but it had been less than 40 minutes from the time I had walked in her door, and only a few minutes since the vision began.

Jane asked if I had reached my goal.

I replied, "It was something much greater."

Then I left.

For the next several days, I spent a lot of time in introspection, sorting out what that whole vision meant. It was, without a doubt, the most intense vision I ever have had in my life.

I tried to make sense of what all the different pieces of the puzzle could represent — the sticks, the fabric, all the children, the guardian, the hands, the ball of fire, the words "plant the seed of light."

For the most part I remained quiet. I didn't want to discuss it with anyone. It was too personal, too private.

As a matter of fact, I didn't share this vision with anyone for a very long time.

(This is the first time ever I have written it all down.)

After several years of keeping it to myself, I chose to share it with only a few people — mostly my students (they always seem to understand).

As time has passed, I have come to believe that this vision was God's way of telling me, "Teach my children."

From that vision, my program "Blessings" evolved.

And since 1994, I have been teaching His children...

*This book is dedicated to the ones I love,
to those who have inspired me,
and to those who have encouraged me
to complete this project:*

my son and his wife,
and my grandchildren,
who keep my heart beating

my parents and my grand-relatives,
who taught me about the important things in life

the very, *very* few people who are my *true* friends
(you know who you are)

all of "MY KIDS"
*who have enriched my life
(you know who you are)*

and most importantly…

my God
who loves me unconditionally

*The awesome girls at the JDC have insisted
that I acknowledge their fabulous ideas and input,
so, thank you, my sweet, lovely girls!*

*Thank you, too, to the boys at the JDC and at the YC
for your suggestions, inspiration, and prayers!*

*To the officers, administration and staff at the facilities
where I have been teaching my program for so many years,
I thank you for your support of my program.
You are truly appreciated.*

*Much love, many blessings and prayers to all of you
for all of your support with this book!*

CONTENTS

PART THREE: THE PRACTICE OF MEDITATION

PART FOUR: CLOSING THOUGHTS

Beloved, if God so loved us,
we ought also to love one another.

– Jesus, in 1 John 4:11

HOW I BEGAN THIS JOURNEY...

Withhold not good from them to whom it is due,
when it is in the power of thine hand to do it.
– Proverbs 3:27

What began on a mountain back when I was a kid in the 60s, took root and began to grow following "The Vision" — and then blossomed in the 90s.

I had begun working as a substitute teacher at a vocational high school in West Central Ohio late in 1989. As a graphic artist and designer by vocation, I substituted primarily in the graphic arts program.

As the owner of a small graphic design and production business, I also served on the graphic arts program's advisory board, and as a judge for their intramural and intermural skills competitions — at both the local and state levels.

When I could work it into my schedule, I would come into the graphic arts lab on occasion to work with students on my own time — mainly because I enjoyed the energy of these kids, and I could see their potential, even if they couldn't. I found it nourished my soul to spend time with these young people and help them to discover their talents.

The Introduction Of Meditation To Students

I began teaching meditation to teenagers in the fall of 1994. I had replaced an instructor in the graphic arts program for a semester, assisting the other program instructor in teaching both the junior and senior classes.

One day, the students asked about the source of my creativity — what I did when I had to create a logo, or brochure, or ad, or whatever, for a client if I wasn't *feeling* very creative. I explained the concept of meditation as a tool to tap into creativity on a subconscious level (more on that in chapter 17).

Those graphic arts students were very interested in the concept, and pushed me to share the art of meditation with them — they asked if I would teach them how it worked.

Since teaching meditation in a school environment was a bit beyond the realm of "normal" at that time, I asked for permission from the supervisor of the program to go forward with a basic meditation class. After explaining in detail what the class would cover, and what I would teach, the supervisor gave me his blessing.

I then taught my first meditation class to teens.

Over the next several years, I was asked to substitute in almost all areas of the school, and on an almost daily basis; I had gotten to know a lot of the students because I was in so many different areas of the school.

Interest in my program increased greatly following that first meditation class. Students talked to their friends about this "very cool thing Mrs. Neal can do," how it was "SO not conventional!" and that it was just for them (not for grown-ups).

They talked to a few of their other teachers about the experience with great enthusiasm, those teachers talked to each other, and they all talked to me.

Fortunately, there were some very enlightened and progressive teachers at that school. As a result, I began presenting the class to students school-wide at the request of those enlightened and progressive teachers. When one of those teachers needed someone to sub for them, they would request me, and would often ask that I present my program to their class.

I was asked to do quite a few presentations at the school for a number of classes and organizations, including the students and staff who were involved in Students Against Destructive Decisions (SADD), the medical and health program students who were studying alternative health practices, and some after-school programs. I also taught my program to students in several of the academic programs, including a Business Leadership class that had a stress management unit as part of its curriculum, and a Senior English class seminar workshop.

As a side note here, my program was voted as one of the top six choices out of the 250 possible topics for seminars the Senior English class wanted to be able to attend at their workshop.

Over time, these wonderful students came up with a name for my program, dubbing it "mrs. neal's not-so-conventional meditation class for teens."

This "not-so-conventional" meditation class has grown over the years into a full, multi-lesson program. Each lesson has been developed as the result of students' questions, requests, curiosity, and eagerness to learn — and from my passion to give students healthy tools to use in their lives.

A Few Years Pass — One Thing Leads To Another...

What I had discovered was that students were hungry for this knowledge; they had lots of questions, and wanted to learn more and more about this meditation program I had been teaching, and the ways it could help them in their lives.

One example:

Following one of my after-school presentations in the spring of 2003, a student came up to me and said that he wished I'd been around when he was locked up in an area juvenile detention center. He had been incarcerated there for a short time and commented, "I really wish I had known how to do this when I was locked up. It would have made it so much easier for me to deal with being there."

His words stuck with me.

I spent several days meditating on his words. If I could do this with the kids at the school, why not share this gift with other kids, too?

I had discovered that this was a wonderful tool I could teach kids to use to help them to stay away from alcohol and drugs as paths of escape, and use something healthy and natural to raise their awareness of their environment, to learn to cope with their every-day struggles, and to *think*.

I contacted the juvenile detention center. After many months of meeting with the administration and explaining what it is I do, they agreed to let me come in periodically to teach the incarcerated youth.

I signed an agreement to follow the policies and procedures of the facility, and to maintain the confidentiality of the youth.

I then began teaching my program at the juvenile detention center. I had received approval for one class every few months; however, because the students enjoyed it so much — and they seemed to be getting so much out of it in a very positive way — the administration asked if I would be willing to come more often. It turned into an every-other-week class.

I have been volunteering at this facility every other Thursday ever since — teaching a one-hour class with the girls, followed by a one-hour class with the boys. Each class includes emphasis on personal responsibility, the mind-body connection, and ways students can use meditation.

This experience led to my teaching at another location a few months later. Several boys had moved from the detention center to a court-ordered youth center, and wanted to continue with my classes. They asked the staff at the youth center to request that I come there to teach, which I gladly agreed to do. About once a month, I go out to see "my kids" at this youth center.

I Love The Phrase, "…And A Child Shall Lead Them…"

Because kids like to talk, word spread about my meditation program, and I soon began teaching at other locations, including several youth centers, schools and a couple of churches.

In 2005, one of my students at the juvenile detention center suggested that I record a CD so he and others could practice meditation when they went home and I wasn't there to guide them. He told me that he could follow along in class when he could hear my voice guiding him, but he had a hard time trying to do a meditation on his own because he kept forgetting how to do it.

After much prayer and meditation, I decided to put a CD together — for my kids. I began by getting input from the students, and deciding what I would include. I sought out the help of a local musician who composed the music for the CD and produced the recording for me.

After recording the first demo, I played it for my girls at the JDC and had them critique it. It was their idea to split it into two tracks — the "Mommy Lectures" and the meditation itself — with their comment, "No offense, Mrs. Neal, we don't want to have to listen to the Mommy Lectures every time we listen to your CD."

It took about a year of research and hard work, but I did it!

To date, hundreds of these CDs have been handed out to kids who are in court-ordered programs — at no cost to them.

Now, A Book — *Just For You*!

One main goal of my program is to give students something to think about.

Meditate = TO THINK.

And so it is with this book: a lot of information to make you think— the same information I present in my classes — all intended to help you understand your *self*: your physical self, your mental self, your spiritual self.

By having this understanding of who you are, and then applying the techniques of meditation I teach in class — or modifying these techniques to what will work for you — you can learn to reduce your stress, deal with your emotions, solve your problems, achieve your goals, change your habits, and yes, even learn more about prayer!

So, because you have asked for it, here is a book filled with the lessons I have been teaching for years.

I would like to point out that you will see some things repeated throughout the book; let's call that a clue — it just might be something that's important and worth repeating.

You will notice, too, that I have added a few pages throughout the book for you to take notes, or to write down your own thoughts and ideas. Make this book your own!

By the way, if you see a word you don't understand, grab a dictionary and look it up!

Kids, this book is designed for *YOU*, to give you the tools you need to find your own personal way to meditate.

It is my hope that you will use this book to help you to find the method that works best for you, and that you will make meditation a part of your daily routine!

I continue to plant the seed of light…

NOTES • THOUGHTS • IDEAS:

NOTES • THOUGHTS • IDEAS:

PART ONE

THE MOMMY LECTURES

Great spirits have always found violent opposition from mediocrities. The latter cannot understand it when a man does not thoughtlessly submit to hereditary prejudices but honestly and courageously uses his intelligence and fulfills the duty to express the results of his thoughts in clear form.

– Albert Einstein, physicist [1]

NOTES • THOUGHTS • IDEAS:

_This drawing is for those of you who will picture me
shaking my finger at you delivering the Mommy lectures..._

AS YOU BEGIN THIS JOURNEY...

Everything is determined, the beginning as well as the end,
by forces over which we have no control.
It is determined for the insect as well as for the star.
Human beings, vegetables or cosmic dust,
we all dance to a mysterious tune,
intoned in the distance by an invisible player.
– Albert Einstein, physicist [2]

I was *that* mother — the one who was always lecturing kids on assorted topics (my own child, as well as other people's children): "That's not healthy for you!" "Go to bed, you need your sleep!" "Look it up!" "You can have water or milk — no soda!" "Do your homework!" and so on. And, I would go into great detail about *why* it was important to get enough sleep, or drink water, or do homework.

Every time I would begin one of my endless lectures, my son would say, "Mom! Please! Not another Mommy Lecture!" He then would comment, "I just asked you what time it is, you don't have to tell me how to build a watch!"

(Apparently, I tend to ramble a bit...)

Looking back, I can see that those Mommy Lectures were the beginning of what would grow into a key part of my program.

Whether he would admit it or not, it helped my son understand when I would explain the "why" — *why* it was important for him to get enough sleep, *why* he had to eat his vegetables, *why* going to school and doing his school work was important, *why* he had to do chores before he could go to a friend's house.

Kids need to know the *whys* and the *hows*.

I found that by explaining *how* and *why* meditation works, and *how* and *why* the body responds to it, kids are more inclined to give it a try, and they will get more of a benefit from it.

I also have found that it has to be the student's choice to participate in any meditation exercise.

Free Will vs. Pre-Destination

There is absolutely no hypnosis or witchcraft involved in any of my classes (believe it or not, I have been asked that question by the skeptics and the critics of my program).

I happen to be a Christian — it's how I was raised.

I believe in pre-destiny, as well as free will.

So, just what is the difference between *pre-destination* and *free will?* I believe pre-destination is the path God has chosen for you. It is that special gift you bring into this world (we all have one); what you are expected to do with your life.

Free will is the gift God has given us that allows us to choose whether we take that path or not, and our right to choose which path we take to get to where we are going.

Here's an example:

Let's say you are pre-destined to become a teacher (pre-destination). You get to choose the path you take to get there (free will).

So, you think about being a teacher when you are a kid, but college seems too expensive and will take so long. Instead, you go to work at a restaurant to pay your bills.

As the years go by, you take a few jobs in sales, then move on to marketing, art and design work.

You start your family, get promoted along the way, start your own business, and have a pretty good life, but that urge to teach is still there.

A position opens up for a substitute teacher at a vocational school, and because of your qualifications — and friendship with the person in charge of hiring — you are offered the position.

You have become a teacher — perhaps not in the conventional manner, but you have achieved your destiny.

An Important Point Here!

Remember that while you *do* get to choose your path in life, you *do not* get to choose anyone else's path! *(More on that topic in chapter seven.)*

I make it a point to tell students that it is always *their choice* whether or not they participate in my class —and to what extent. I believe strongly in free will, and that I do take away *anyone's* free will — no one has that right.

So, What *Is* Meditation?

Rid your mind of any pre-conceived notions you may have about meditation (believe me, I have heard them all). There are as many methods of practicing meditation as there are people who do it, and just as many reasons to do it.

Basically, it is putting oneself into a state of deep relaxation to allow for mindfulness.

Meditation is a very personal experience.

The method presented in my program, and in this book, is just one of many; I developed this method and have used it for years because it works well with young people.

What Exactly Does It Mean To Meditate?

Look it up! The definition according to the dictionary:

meditate [L. *meditari*, to consider.]

to consider thoughtfully; to intend;

to ponder, especially on religious matters.

Simply put, meditation is *thinking*.

It is an exercise of contemplation which can be used to train, calm, focus or empty the mind. It is a method of achieving an altered state without the use of any chemical substances.

It allows you to stay in control of your mind and your body at all times. With meditation, you do not hand over control of *you* to any *one* or any *thing* at any time.

You will see the word "think" a lot in this book. When you see the word "think" as you read this book, think "meditate."

How Can You Use Meditation?

You can choose to use meditation techniques just to relax, to help you sleep, to gain insight, to help you study, or to use the power of your subconscious mind to achieve goals, change habits, solve problems, or to pray. Meditation can be an *intense* form of prayer!

It sometimes takes a bit of patience and practice to reach a meditative state. As with anything else, the more you practice, the easier it becomes as you condition your brain and body to work together to reach this state.

Once you have experienced this state of mind and body, *you* get to choose how you want to use it.

THINK TIME:

How will you choose to use meditation?

NOTES • THOUGHTS • IDEAS:

NOTES • THOUGHTS • IDEAS:

MAINTAIN A HEALTHY BODY...

The wise man should consider that
health is the greatest of human blessings.
Let food be your medicine.
– Hippocrates, father of medicine

You have been amazingly created!

God has placed within you all you need to soothe your spirit and calm your soul. All you have to do is learn how to tap into what He has given you.

An important part of making that connection is to keep your body and your mind healthy.

You always should be aware of what you are allowing into your body — physically, mentally, and spiritually — including the types of food and drink, music, movies, and the influence of your family and friends.

Physical Health

Part of taking care of your body is to be sure you are eating properly, drinking plenty of water, and getting plenty of rest.

The types of food you choose to put into your body can make a huge difference to your overall health.

Nutrition is an important part of keeping your stress levels under control by making sure you maintain a healthy body.

Be aware of the foods you eat — eat your veggies, stay away from sugars and unhealthy fats, and avoid junk food!

Basically, natural foods — foods that are not processed — are best for you. As my doctor tells me, shop the outer aisles of the store and try to stay away from the center aisles.

Learn to read labels, and know what you are putting into your body. If you are not sure what kinds of food are healthiest for you — look it up!

True Story:

When my son was a teenager, one of his friends — we'll call him Michael — came by our house on a Sunday morning to pick him up. The two boys had plans for the day that involved their trucks and mud.

We had just finished our breakfast which had included a little bacon (an occasional weekend treat), and the pan with the bacon grease was still on the stove.

Michael had some sort of big dripping-with-grease fast-food sandwich and a huge order of fries in one hand, and held a very large soda in his other hand when he came to the door looking for my son.

He mentioned he needed to stop and get gas before they continued with their plans for the day.

This brought on the "mommy lecture" on nutrition.

I asked Michael if he cared even a little bit about what he was putting into his body, then proceeded to tell him the importance of eating food that was good for him, and the dangers of drinking so much soda — he said this was his second one of the day.

Like many teens, he didn't seem to care all that much about the nutritional value — or lack thereof — of his meal.

Then I asked, "Since you need fuel for your truck, would you like to use this left-over bacon grease?"

He looked at me with a look of shock and horror on his face!

He said quite emphatically that he would *never* put any bacon grease into *his* truck!

I smiled and said, "So, you care more about what you put into your truck than what you are putting into your body?"

Point made.

The bottom line is you cannot separate your mind from your body. Poor nutrition can contribute to elevated levels of stress — not to mention poor health, which also contributes to elevated levels of stress. *(The good news is, one of the benefits of meditation is that it helps to reduce stress.)*

The Importance Of ... WATER!

> *Beloved, I wish above all things that thou mayest prosper*
> *and be in health, even as thy soul prospereth.*
> – 3 John 1:2

Another aspect of maintaining a healthy body — and topic of another Mommy Lecture — is the importance of avoiding less-than-healthy beverages, and drinking enough water.

Question: Do you know how much of your body is made up of water, and how much of your brain is made up of water?

Answer: On average, the human body is comprised of from 66% to 75% water (or at least 2/3 of your body weight). Your brain is comprised of about 85% to 90% water.

Some Facts About Your Body And Water...

You lose, on average, about 2.5 quarts of water each day.

Let's do some math!

How many ounces are in 2.5 quarts?

(Hint, one quart is 32 ounces.)

32 + 32 +16 = 80

So how many glasses of water do you need to replace that 80 ounces or so you lose every day?

If an average sized drinking glass is about 10 ounces, in order to replace the water you lose, you should drink *(on average)* eight of those 10-ounce glasses of water daily.

This amount may vary based on your age, sex, level of activity, and body type.

Interesting Stuff You Just Might Like...

- You can't count other beverages — such as soda, coffee, tea, juice, etc. — because they contain substances that contradict the effects of water, and actually can dehydrate you and deplete nutrients from your body.
- Your body loses water whether you are awake or asleep from the moisture in your breath, and through your skin in the form of perspiration. In addition, you lose water from your body through urination, crying, talking, spitting, and drooling.
- You should be drinking water throughout the day. If you wait until you're thirsty to get a drink of water, you will already have lost 16 or more ounces of your total body water.
- When you aren't drinking enough water to keep yourself hydrated, your body will retain water to compensate. The more water you drink, the less water you retain.

- There is such a thing as drinking too much water which can have a negative impact on your overall health. If you are not sure how much is good for *you*, ask your doctor.

Student Tip:

Drinking water helps the brain function more efficiently; take a drink of water before your next test!

The Importance Of ... SLEEP!

Sleep is the best meditation.
– His Holiness Tenzin Gyatso, Dalai Lama

I often ask my students how much sleep they get each night. Most tell me they get less than six hours of sleep per night; not nearly what they should be getting.

Statistically, we are a sleep-deprived country — one-third of *all* Americans get six hours or less of sleep per night.

With everything you have going on in your life — including school work and extracurricular activities at school (sports, band, theater, clubs, etc.), homework, studying and tests, jobs, household chores, playing video and/or computer games, hanging out with friends, texting, chatting, and so on — you are staying active from the time you get up until the time you get to bed, and you rarely get enough sleep.

Getting enough sleep is necessary in order to maintain good health. This is when healing of your brain and body occurs.

During sleep, the body secretes a hormone that repairs and regenerates tissue throughout the body.

Research indicates that on average — based on your age — you need the following number of hours of sleep per night:

YOUR AGE:	SLEEP YOU NEED:
1-2 years of age	14-15 hours
3-5 years of age	10-12 hours
6-10 years of age	10 hours
12-18 years of age	8-9 hours
19-65 years of age	7-8 hours
65 + years of age	7-8 hours

Sleep is defined in two ways: the number of hours you sleep and the quality of your sleep. When you don't get enough sleep, it can affect your physical and mental performance throughout the day.

Many factors can interfere with the sleep process.

The "stress response" causes adrenaline to be released into your system, which will prevent you from falling asleep.

Nicotine has a similar effect on the body as caffeine; both are stimulants that can interfere with sleep. Those who don't sleep well — or who don't spend enough time sleeping — may suffer all day from feeling irritable, anxious, and less able to focus, as well as having memory problems and a short attention span.

Some other effects include impaired alertness and reasoning skills, a lack of concentration and problem solving skills, overeating, depression, and a slowed reaction time which could be particularly hazardous when driving.

Chronic sleep loss also can affect your health in a number of ways including increased stress levels, and a higher risk for high blood pressure, diabetes and heart disease.

Meditation — and the relaxation response — can *help* with the sleep process. It can be a great tool for getting into a relaxed state, leading to peaceful and restorative sleep.

Sleep Cycles

The sleep process includes two sleep states: REM (rapid eye movement) and NREM (non-rapid eye movement).

The cycle usually begins with a period of about 80 minutes of deep NREM sleep (Delta) followed by about 10 minutes of REM (Theta) sleep. This 90-minute cycle is repeated four to six times each night.

If this sequence is interrupted, the quality of sleep suffers.

You should have several periods of deep, restorative non-rapid eye movement (NREM) sleep, and four to five cycles of rapid eye movement (REM) sleep each night. Deep NREM sleep is vital in maintaining general health; it accounts for longer periods of sleep during which our brain activity and bodily functions slow down. REM happens in brief spurts of increased activity in the brain and body, and is considered the dreaming stage of sleep.

The periods of REM sleep get longer as the night progresses. Studies have shown that between the seventh and eighth hour is when you get almost an hour of REM sleep. REM affects our moods, performance and behavior by processing learning and memory, and resolving emotional distress.

Interesting Stuff You Just Might Like...
- When you meditate — or go to sleep — you reach a state where your body and mind are calm and quiet. Your brain releases endorphins to relax you. You may feel that your body

is asleep or detached — this is called sleep paralysis, or pseudo paralysis.

- Everybody dreams — several times a night — however, we don't always remember our dreams.
- Dreams that occur earlier in the sleep cycle will be shorter, and the dreams that occur later in the sleep cycle will be longer. Dreams last anywhere from just a few seconds up to as long as 30 minutes or so; most people only remember the dream they had just before waking.
- Not everyone dreams in color.

Student Tip*:*

To help ensure you get enough sleep, have a sleep schedule; get up each day and go to bed each night at the same time.

The Importance Of … BREATHING!

Breath is the bridge which connects life to consciousness,
which unites your body to your thoughts.
– Thích Nhất Hạnh, Vietnamese Zen Monk

Breathing is the single most important thing you do from the moment you are born until the moment you die. And, it is a key element in relaxation and in the practice of meditation.

So, do you think you know how to breathe?

You're probably thinking, "Yes, of course I do!"

Let's find out.

Place one hand on your chest and one on your stomach. Take a few breaths. Be honest. Are you breathing deeply — can you feel the hand on your stomach moving? Or are you just *panting* — breathing with only the top part of your lungs?

Now, bring your *awareness* to your breathing.

Really pay attention to *how* you breathe.

When you take a breath, you should relax your belly muscles so you can breathe deeply to fill your lungs.

Breathing is a natural physical reflex to stress, and one that can help with relaxation.

Just a few breaths will trigger the "relaxation response" — the opposite of the "stress response" — sending a message for the brain to release chemicals which help us to relax.

Try it! Sit up straight, relax your shoulders, close your eyes, and take a few deep breaths. Inhale deeply through your nose. Be aware of how it feels when the air is going in your nose and filling your lungs. Exhale slowly, controlling your breath as you exhale. Be aware of how you feel as your breath leaves your body.

You should notice your body relaxing a little with each breath you take.

The Nose Is For Breathing, The Mouth Is For Eating

There are several benefits to breathing through your nose.

The nostrils and sinuses not only filter and warm the air going into the lungs, but breathing through your nose also will lessen your chance of catching a cold.

The mucous membrane lining the nose extends from the nostrils, through the trachea, on to the bronchi, then directly into the lungs. The mucous catches and kills the germs, keeping you healthier!

Your nasal passages have many nerve endings and when you take a breath, air rushes past those nerve endings and sends a message to your brain — you are stimulating the calming centers of the brain. So, next time you are stressed, take a breath!

Interesting Stuff You Just Might Like...

- Most adults in the U.S., about 90% of them, are "shallow breathers," breathing only into the chest, not breathing deeply into the lungs. This causes the bottom 1/3 of the lungs to become like dead space.
- Children, however — and most mammals — are naturally-born belly breathers. Have you ever watched babies, or puppies, or kittens when they are sleeping? Their little bellies are moving as they breathe.
- Men average 12 to 14 breaths per minute (bpm), women average 13 to 15 bpm, and children average 15 to 18 bpm.
- The sinuses produce nitric oxide (NO) which is a pollutant but harmful to bacteria in small doses.
- Breathing through your mouth increases the loss of body hydration (water), which ties in with the importance of drinking water throughout the day.

A Little Trivia:

On average, man may be able to survive
40 days without food, perhaps 4 days without water,
but only 4 minutes without air.

THINK TIME:

Are you aware of what you put into your body?
Do you get enough sleep? Drink enough water?
Do you take a breath when you're stressed?

NOTES • THOUGHTS • IDEAS:

NOTES • THOUGHTS • IDEAS:

CHAPTER THREE

MAINTAIN A HEALTHY MIND

The mind is an iceberg — it floats with only
one-seventh of its bulk above water.
– Sigmund Freud, psycho-analyst

Doing things to keep your mind healthy and fit is just as important as doing things to keep your body healthy and fit. Mental exercise is as important as physical exercise; more about that in chapter 21.

For now, we're just going to talk about your mind. While meditation can be a wonderful tool that you can use to help you to keep yourself mentally healthy and fit, *understanding your mind* also can play an important role in mental fitness.

You have in your possession an amazing and powerful tool that you can use at any time you choose to use it — that tool is your subconscious mind!

Let's take some time to discuss this super power of yours...

The Power Of The Subconscious Mind

Generally speaking, when you study psychology — the study of the psyche, or mind — you are introduced to the father of psycho-analysis, Sigmund Freud, and his concept of the division of the human psyche into the id, ego and superego.

Basically, the id represents the basic biological urges such as hunger, thirst, etc.; those body systems controlled by the subconscious mind. The ego directs and controls those urges with conscious action, and the superego is referred to as the moral part of the personality, or the conscience.

Carl Jung, a world-renowned psycho-analyst and a friend of Freud's, posed the concept of the collective unconscious.

Basically, this collective unconscious is a collective "knowing" — a knowledge that all human beings share — that is accessed through our dreams and visions. Jung placed a lot of focus on the symbols in dreams (more on *that* in chapter 23), embracing the symbolism of the *self*, rather than on the literal translation of the symbols.

HOMEWORK ASSIGNMENT!

Study the work of these two men *(Freud and Jung)* to gain a bit of insight into the complexity and limitless possibilities of your mind.

The Basics — How All Of This Relates To Meditation

There are things we do, decisions we make, and actions we take on a conscious level, and there are things that we do that are directed on a subconscious level.

Our conscious mind is in the here and now, aware of the phenomena and events within and outside of ourselves.

Your subconscious mind is the keeper of knowledge. Everything you have ever read, heard, seen, learned — it's all stored in your subconscious mind; this is where you can find the answers to your challenges.

You can access your subconscious mind through meditation.

Think of it like the operating system of a computer that holds knowledge. You just have to know how to use it!

When you are in a relaxed state — like during meditation — your subconscious is open to the suggestions you choose to feed into it. When you reach this point, you can think about the goals you want to achieve, the habits you want to change, the problems you want to solve, the prayers you want to send — *you* choose.

When you keep your conscious mind occupied with high expectations and goals, you allow the subconscious mind to reproduce your habitual thinking, or to manifest the reality you want or expect.

Conscious Mind vs. Subconscious Mind

One key difference between the conscious mind and the subconscious mind is that the subconscious mind does not distinguish between what is real and what is not real. To your subconscious mind, everything is real.

The subconscious mind never sleeps, nor does it ever rest. It is always turned on, always processing, always taking in information that is being fed in to it.

The subconscious mind does not think for itself; it only reacts to input it receives. It processes what is fed into it as "real" — one reason children have nightmares — and it will work to make "correct" any input it receives.

When you watch a movie, listen to a song, or play a computer or video game, your subconscious mind "believes" that what you are experiencing is reality.

Think of your subconscious mind as a garden that you want to plant. *You* hold the key to planting the seeds into your subconscious that you want to grow — that you want to harvest into your life.

When you plant positive, harmonious, and encouraging seeds — or thoughts — you harvest a positive, harmonious and encouraging result. However, if you fill your mind with negativity, you will reap negativity.

Whatever you allow into your subconscious will be perceived as real. This is one explanation of why visualization during meditation works. (More on visualization in chapter 15.)

Note that when you are in a meditative state, your subconscious mind may bring forward ideas, solutions, images, etc.

For you creative people (artists, writers, musicians, etc.), it is a good idea to keep a pencil and paper close by for note-taking — either for meditation, or when you sleep. If you wait until you are fully awake, these thoughts will be gone. (Read more on this topic in chapter 17.)

Through meditation, you more easily tap into the unlimited power of your subconscious mind. Remember, *you* get to decide how you use this tool.

Interesting Stuff You Just Might Like...

- The subconscious mind controls the autonomic body systems.
- It is important always be on guard; be aware of what you allow to get into your subconscious mind in the form of music, television, movies, video or computer games, etc.

THINK TIME:

> *How can you use your subconscious to achieve goals,*
> *change habits, solve problems, or send prayers?*

NOTES • THOUGHTS • IDEAS:

_____

CHAPTER FOUR

PRAYERFUL MEDITATION AND SPIRITUAL HEALTH

Give us this day our daily bread.

– Jesus, in Matthew 6:11

This is one of my favorite Mommy Lectures to teach — the importance of Spiritual Health.

I frequently mention the power of prayer in class. I do believe strongly in the power of prayer. I begin each day in meditative prayer; without it, I cannot do what I do.

A student once commented to me, "So, how are we supposed to pray? I've never learned how to do that."

I smiled.

From that one comment from that one student, a whole class on prayer evolved.

His question was an easy one to answer; Jesus, the Christ, had supplied the answer.

I pulled out my Bible, which I just happened to have with me that evening — and, of course, it was a "coincidence" that I happened to have it with me.

A favorite reading adventure of mine is reading the Gospels; I am particularly fond of Luke. I opened my Bible to Luke 11:1-4 and read to the class:

¹ And it came to pass, that, as he was praying in a certain place, when he ceased, one of his disciples said unto him, Lord, teach us to pray, as John also taught his disciples.

² And he said unto them, When ye pray, say, Our Father which art in heaven, Hallowed be thy name. Thy kingdom come. Thy will be done, as in heaven, so in earth.
³ Give us day by day our daily bread.
⁴ And forgive us our sins; for we also forgive every one that is indebted to us. And lead us not into temptation; but deliver us from evil.

While there were several students who recognized this as *The Lord's Prayer*, it made me more than a little sad that quite a few students didn't know what it was. How sad that so many young people don't know how to pray — they either never have been taught, or they never have been exposed to any practice of faith.

The next question was expected, "Do we have to memorize all that to pray right?"

Again, I smiled.

"No," I answered. "This is how we are taught to pray; this is the format Jesus gave to us for prayer. You just follow this format and speak to God from your heart.

"Think of God as the PERFECT parent, and when you speak to Him, trust that He loves you — *no matter what."*

There are variations of this prayer, depending on the version of the Bible you use and whether you refer to Luke's or Matthew's version; but the format is the same.

For example, Matthew's version in some Bibles includes the doxology, *"For Thine is the kingdom and the power and the glory forever. Amen."*

I then shared Matthew, Chapter 6:1-13, as it goes into a deeper explanation of prayer and how to pray.

I have included verses 1-4 here because they explain the importance of keeping what you do to yourself, and not performing for others. The verses refer to charitable giving (alms) — this can be food, money, or other donations given to needy people — and express that we are not to put our giving of alms on display for the world to see.

Prayer, as well, should be personal, private — not something you do to show off in front of others.

> *¹ Take heed that ye do not your alms before men, to be seen of them: otherwise ye have no reward of your Father which is in heaven.*
>
> *² Therefore when thou doest thine alms, do not sound a trumpet before thee, as the hypocrites do in the synagogues and in the streets, that they may have glory of men. Verily I say unto you, They have their reward.*
>
> *³ But when thou doest alms, let not thy left hand know what thy right hand doeth:*
>
> *⁴ That thine alms may be in secret: and thy Father which seeth in secret himself shall reward thee openly.*
>
> *⁵ And when thou prayest, thou shalt not be as the hypocrites are: for they love to pray standing in the synagogues and in the corners of the streets, that they may be seen of men. Verily I say unto you, They have their reward.*
>
> *⁶ But thou, when thou prayest, enter into thy closet, and when thou hast shut thy door, pray to thy Father which is in secret; and thy Father which seeth in secret shall reward thee openly.*
>
> *⁷ But when ye pray, use not vain repetitions, as the heathen do: for they think that they shall be heard for their much speaking.*
>
> *⁸ Be not ye therefore like unto them: for your Father knoweth what things ye have need of, before ye ask him.*
>
> *⁹ After this manner therefore pray ye: Our Father which art in heaven, Hallowed be thy name.*

[10] *Thy kingdom come. Thy will be done in earth, as it is in heaven.*

[11] *Give us this day our daily bread.*

[12] *And forgive us our debts, as we forgive our debtors.*

[13] *And lead us not into temptation, but deliver us from evil: For thine is the kingdom, and the power, and the glory, for ever. Amen.*

Break It Down...

Let's discuss this format for prayer — line-by-line — using *The Lord's Prayer:*

"Our Father which art in Heaven, Hallowed be thy name."

As in any conversation, you first address the Father. Call on Him and praise His name. Confirm that His name is above all others; that it is holy.

"Thy kingdom come. Thy will be done in earth, as it is in heaven."

Let Him know you want His kingdom — His rulership — to come to pass, and you want His will to be the same here on earth as it is in heaven — that you want life here on earth to be as wonderful as it is in heaven.

"Give us this day our daily bread."

Ask Him for what it is you want, or need from Him — your daily bread. Bread can represent so many things — nutritional sustenance, food for the soul, or even money...

"And forgive us our debts, as we forgive our debtors."

Forgiveness is a biggie (and one, I admit, I struggle with on a daily basis). We ask for His forgiveness, which we receive by grace and through His love; however, just as we receive forgiveness, we are expected to forgive those who have caused us harm. As we forgive, so are we forgiven.

"And lead us not into temptation, but deliver us from evil:"

Ask for His guidance and protection from the temptation to do something we know is wrong, for help in staying on our path, and for His protection from the evil one — Satan.

"For thine is the kingdom, and the power, and the glory, for ever."

This phrase is the doxology, or "praise phrase," that appears in Mark's version of this scripture. Recognize God's supreme power, and give praise to Him, now and forever.

"Amen."

Customarily, this is considered the closing to a prayer. It is a word that signifies agreement or confirmation, and is used in worship by all three of the Abrahamic faiths (Jews, Christians, and Muslims).

Sum It Up...

The point is, prayer does not have to be complicated or formal, nor does it have to have a lot of big words or be said with intensity. Prayer should be a sincere and heart-felt conversation with our Father, God.

Following the format Jesus the Christ gave us, we speak from our hearts directly to the heart of God.

A prayer can be as simple as, "Dear Lord, please help me." He hears our prayers, and He always answers them. Learn to watch and listen for the answer. It can be something as simple as someone crossing your path at just the moment you need them.

As a Christian, I have faith — I believe my prayers always will be answered. The answer may not be what I want — or what I expect — but it is always the right answer.

I always close my prayers — because I believe what I read in the Bible — with the words, "In Jesus' name I pray. Amen,"

YOU Decide Who Wins!

I mentioned in class one night that the best way to fight the darkness is to shine a light on it — or to turn on the light. One of the boys in class said, "Mrs. Neal, you need to make sure you include that in your book."

This seems like a good place to mention it! Prayer and being positive just seem to go together.

Rather than dwelling on the negative — or bad, or evil — try to focus on the positive and good things in your life.

Count your blessings *(I say that a lot, too)*. Always.

And pray. Always.

Not to get *too* preachy here, but when you choose to stay focused on the negative things in your life, evil wins. Satan is after your soul and will use whatever means he can to win it.

I encourage students to try to see the bright side of any situation — or at least a *brighter* side — and not focus on the dark.

Recognize that we *all* have challenges in life — but we also have been given a gift or two. Spend a little time in quiet meditative prayer, and find your gift.

THINK TIME:

Pray. Have a personal and heart-felt conversation with God...

NOTES • THOUGHTS • IDEAS:

NOTES • THOUGHTS • IDEAS:

YOUR MORAL COMPASS — WHO INFLUENCES YOURS?

And whether one member suffer, all the members suffer with it;
or one member be honoured, all the members rejoice with it.

1 Corinthians 12:26

Anyone — or anything — that serves to help guide your decisions based on morals or virtues is part of your Moral Compass.

Your Moral Compass is what influences you to choose to do what you do, and to behave the way you behave.

From that moment when you were conceived, your environment began to influence who you would become.

(I will not get into a debate here about when life begins — this comment is based on my personal beliefs, with no apologies).

After you were born, and as you have continued to grow, the people who have been in your life have taught you about "normal" behavior. They — along with the other sensory influences in your life — have helped to set your Moral Compass.

From Whom Have You Learned Your Morals?

While everything in your environment has an effect on you, the people who are closest to you have the greatest influence.

Think about the people in your life.

Who are *your* role models? Who do *you* look up to?

Think about the influence these people have had on you and how they have helped to shape your ideas, opinions, ethics, values and morals.

Anyone can be a positive — or, not-so-positive — role model. Go beyond family and friends, and include anyone you may encounter or anyone who influences you in any way — your teachers, your spiritual leader (rabbi, pastor, priest, minister), a community leader, your parents' friends, a singer, actor, athlete or other celebrity, even the cashier at the grocery store.

Think about how these people have influenced you.

Think about the movies, TV programs, or sports you watch, or the video games you play, or the music you listen to — and think about the people who are part of that entertainment culture.

Positive Role Model...

Positive role models tend to have a lot in common. They work for the greater good to make their community a better place, they are compassionate and are committed to what they do, they are able to achieve the goals they set, they have set high standards for themselves, they have good ethics, and they are admired for their strength and courage, and their ability to be a good influence on those around them.

Think about it.

Who might you know who fits the description of a *positive* role model?

...or Not?

While there are plenty of really good role models, there are also a lot of not-so-good role models and — unfortunately — they can have a strong influence in your life, too.

Think about that female singer who feels the need to get up on a stage wearing barely more than underwear, and gyrate obscenely to get any attention she can get.

This has nothing to do with her singing talent — this is a gimmick to boost sales of her albums, perfume, clothing line, and so on. She wants your money.

Period.

This is someone I absolutely would *not* suggest my students look up to as a positive role model.

This singer might be a nice enough person — she may go to church every Sunday, and help the poor every chance she gets. However, the image she projects while performing is the one that young people will see, and this is the image they will remember and emulate.

Now, how about that athlete who is being paid millions of dollars to play a game, and chooses to spend his millions on drugs, alcohol, and partying at his huge house — and only places value on those material things?

Again, this is not someone I would suggest as a positive role model.

He, too, may be a nice person who volunteers at homeless shelters and visits kids in hospitals. However, the image young people see is that guy wearing all the bling with half-dressed girls hanging on him. This is what impresses young people, influences them, and helps to set their Moral Compasses.

Think about the people you look up to as role models. What are their priorities? If they are interested only in how much money they can get you to spend buying their products and supporting them, are they really worthy of your time and attention?

Are they worthy of the honor of having such an influence in your life?

What *Is* Celebrity All About, Anyway?

While I'm on this topic, here's something else for you to think about: why are these people (the "celebrities") being elevated to a "royal" status? What, exactly have they done that is so extraordinary that they should be worshipped by the masses?

Think about the people you know in your community who are hard-working and dedicated, and who do their jobs well.

What makes "celebrities" different from those people in your community? What makes them more important, more worthy of attention?

And, again, are they truly worthy of the honor of helping to set anyone's Moral Compass?

Now, Let's Take This One Step Further...

Think about this for a minute: just as you have role models who have helped you to set your Moral Compass; there are those whose Moral Compass you help to set.

Do you have a child of your own, or younger siblings, or cousins, nieces or nephews? How about that kid next door? Or that little kid who lives down the street and follows you around all the time? You know the one I mean — that one who thinks you are just *the coolest kid ever*?

You may not have signed up for it, and you may not want the responsibility of being a role model, but — like it or not — you are a role model to someone in your life.

The next time you find yourself in the presence of any younger kids, be aware of your behavior, your language, even how you dress.

Just as you have been influenced by others, you are in a position to have an influence on others.

Whether you are looking up to someone, or someone is looking up to you, choose wisely when you are setting your Moral Compass.

THINK TIME:

Who are you allowing to influence you,
and are they worthy of that honor?

NOTES • THOUGHTS • IDEAS:

CHAPTER SIX

HOW WE IMPACT EACH OTHER'S LIVES

Ye are the light of the world.
A city that is set on an hill cannot be hid.
Neither do men light a candle, and put it under a bushel, but
on a candlestick; and it giveth light unto all that are in the house.
– Matthew 5:14-15

I ask students which of the following is correct:

a) what you do is your business and it doesn't matter to anyone because you aren't affecting anyone else, and what you do doesn't matter anyway,

or

b) everything you do impacts someone else.

The good news is, most of them know that the correct answer is "b." The bad news is, they sometimes want to believe the correct answer is "a."

Our lives are all connected.

Did you read that last chapter about role models?

It doesn't matter who you are, the choices you make in your life will impact many lives around you — the decisions you make, the things you do or say, even what you wear.

And, you touch more lives than you may realize.

The Ripple Effect of One Action...

Let's think about an average day of an average student. She gets up in the morning, gets ready for school, eats breakfast, and heads out the door. She sees a family photo on the desk as she is leaving, and starts thinking about her grandfather and the birthday dinner her mom is going to make for him that evening.

On her way to school, she sees an old man who is having a hard time getting across the street. No one stops to help him, not even her.

When she gets to school, she still is thinking about that old man, and at lunch time, she tells her friends about him.

Now her friends are thinking about that old man, too.

They all get together after school, and make plans to stop by a local shelter on the weekend to see if they can volunteer to help there — secretly hoping they might run into that old man.

That weekend, four students show up at the shelter and volunteer their time. It becomes a regular thing for two of them, volunteering every other weekend.

How many lives do you think were impacted in this little story, and how did it all start? What was it that sparked the idea of volunteering to help at the shelter?

Was it perhaps the mother's plan to make a birthday dinner for the grandfather that started this chain of events? Was it the family photo that the girl glanced at as she walked out the door? Or was it that the girl had been thinking of her grandfather when she noticed the old man crossing the street — would she have noticed the old man crossing the street had she not been thinking of her grandfather? Or, did the girl feel guilty about not helping the old man cross the street? Is that what affected her enough to tell her friends, and to get them to volunteer at the shelter with her?

Let's take a look at what happened here: the grandfather, the mother, the daughter, the old man, and the friends at school all were impacting each other's lives, not to mention the impact on the lives of the people at the shelter.

Even though the girls never ran into the old man, something started them on the path to having an impact on other peoples' lives.

Because one girl's life was changed by watching an old man trying to get across a street, the lives of people at a shelter also were changed.

The Butterfly Effect

In chaos theory, there is a phenomenon known as *The Butterfly Effect;* this relates to cause and effect — the origin of an outcome.

I love this very simplistic explanation: "a butterfly flapping its pretty little wings at the equator can start a breeze that will grow into a wind, and eventually will create a hurricane on the other side of the globe."

In much the same way, our words, our actions, and our choices have an effect on everyone we encounter — and sometimes, it has a ripple effect.

We impact and change each other's lives simply by being a part of each other's lives.

As my mother once said to me, "Choose your words wisely. Be careful what you say, you don't know how far your words will travel."

Don't you think the same applies to actions?

THINK TIME:

How have your choices impacted the lives of those around you?

CHAPTER SEVEN

RESPECTING EACH OTHER'S PERSONAL PATH

If a man does not keep pace with his companions,
perhaps it is because he hears a different drummer.
Let him step to the music which he hears,
however measured or far away.
– Henry David Thoreau, author

So, we've talked about your role models, and about the impact we all have on each other's lives.

Now let's talk about personal "choices" — the control we have over which path we choose to take, or not to take.

And, what control we have over which path someone else is choosing to take, or not to take.

It's natural to want to point out each other's flaws — to tell someone else what they should or should not be doing — and it's hard to resist offering a friend a few suggestions on how to fix their lives. (There's a nice Biblical reference on this topic in the book of Matthew, chapter seven — look it up.)

If only our friends would listen to us!

When you feel that urge to tell your friend what path they should be choosing, take a step back, and take a breath.

Remember that whole free will thing I talked about back in chapter one? And, how God may have a plan for us (pre-destination), but we get to choose how we get from where we currently are in our life to where we are going in our life (free will)?

The truth is, we have no control whatsoever over what other people choose to do (or not to do) with their lives — or which path they choose to take (or not take).

We only get to choose our own path. We don't have any control over anyone else's. It's their choice, and theirs alone.

People are going to think whatever they want to think, and they will say whatever they want to say — you have no control over any of that.

> *All you get to control is how you react or respond to*
> *what is going on around you, and how you allow it to affect you.*

As much as I would love to tell my students what they should or should not be doing with their lives — and how they should or should not be doing it — I don't have that right.

Neither do you.

A Different Perspective

You know that you would not appreciate it if someone else — even a close friend — tried to tell you what to do with your life.

We all have had different role models, different backgrounds, different environments, different friends, and different influences that have shaped who we are.

We each have walked a different path that has brought us to this particular point in time.

Your life experiences are unique to you — you are the only one who has lived your life.

You should respect the choices your friends make, whether you agree with them or not. It's their choice, it's their decision, it's their path to choose — free will.

Just remember, you can offer them guidance or help, but you can't make the choice of which path to take for them.

The Exception...

Pay attention here. There are exceptions to this!

I am not referring to when you see someone making a questionable fashion choice — I am talking about the serious stuff — the life and liberty choices.

I am *not* suggesting that you should look the other way — or remain silent — if you see a friend making choices that could be harmful to their health, or dangerous, or illegal.

If you care about that person even a little, you should speak up — say something to them, or to someone else.

I tell students all the time, "I respect your rights, but if I see you doing something that will harm you or someone else, I will turn you in — in a heartbeat!"

I *absolutely* do not subscribe to that concept of *"omerta"* (look it up) when it comes to the safety of kids.

Neither should you.

Get A Little Self-Centered

It's okay to question someone's motivation when they try to get you to do something that you know is not going to be a good choice for you. Ask yourself, "What's their motivation for trying to get me to do this with them/for them? And, what's the possible consequence?"

Here's the self-centered part: always make *your* choices for *you*. Don't allow someone else to make those choices for you.

Here's an example of what this means:

Let's say you are in class and your best friend asks you to join in a school-wide protest he has organized because the school has eliminated peanut butter sandwiches from the lunch menu.

You love peanut butter sandwiches, and you feel a little sad that the school is no longer going to have them on the menu.

The protest that is planned includes everyone getting up and walking out of class at exactly 10:45 a.m., and lying on the lunchroom floor until the last lunch period is over at 1:00 p.m.

You will be in your math class at 10:45 a.m., taking an important test, and you will be presenting your science project with your lab partner at 11:30 a.m.

Your parents already have told you that if your grades don't come up, you will be grounded for life.

You have plans to go to a surprise birthday party for your girlfriend on Saturday, and if you are grounded for life, you won't be able to go.

If you walk out of the math class and skip the science class, you will fail both classes and your grades will not go up.

If you do not participate in the protest, your best friend who has planned this protest probably will never speak to you again.

If you get grounded and can't attend your girlfriend's surprise party, she probably will never speak to you again.

What do you do?

Tough one, isn't it?

I can't answer this one — this is something you will have to figure out.

You have to decide what's best for *you.*

Regardless of which decision you make, you have to respect your friends' decisions, and they have to respect yours.

THINK TIME:

How are you reacting or responding to what is going on around you?

How are you allowing it to affect you?

NOTES • THOUGHTS • IDEAS:

PART TWO

THE HOWs and WHYs
and OTHER LESSONS

Science is not only compatible with spirituality;
it is a profound source of spirituality.
– Carl Sagan, scientist / astronomer

NOTES • THOUGHTS • IDEAS:

THE PHYSIOLOGY and SCIENCE BEHIND MEDITATION

The world is but a canvas to the imagination.
– Henry David Thoreau, author

Now, About That Brain Of Yours...

Have you ever slowed your brain waves down?

What does *that* mean?

It's nothing weird, or "woo-woo," or magical or mystical — *this is a trick question.* The answer is, all of us slow our brain waves down — it's something that happens every time we are in a relaxed state, or when we go to sleep.

How This Works...

The brain is an electrochemical organ that vibrates similarly to the way the heart beats, but more rapidly.

The normal resting heart rate for the human heart is between 60-100 beats per minute (averaging between 72-80); the average brain — when a person is fully awake — normally vibrates from 20-22 cycles per second (cps), or hertz (Hz). This refers to the number of times a brain wave repeats itself within one second.

This rate of 20-22 cps would be the mid-range of the beta frequencies (more on that later in this chapter). Research has shown that people who have highly-stressed, fast-paced lives have much higher *average* vibrations — well above 25 cps.

The brain vibrations, or the electrical activity emanating from the brain, also are known as brain wave frequencies. Have you ever watched a movie or television program that showed a person in a hospital bed with electrodes and wires attached to their head, and a monitor showing the "blips" of the brain activity? Those "blips" are measuring brain wave frequencies.

Brain Wave Frequencies And Their cps/Hz:

Listed below are the different brain wave frequencies, along with their cps, or Hz, and a brief description of the physical effects you may experience in each frequency's state.

- **GAMMA*** (greater than 30 Hz / up to 100+ Hz) — Associated with precognition, hyper-awareness, panic, anger, high-level information processing. At this frequency level, stress hormones (cortisol, epinephrine, etc.) are released into the body, which are harmful to health.

  * Equipment had to be specially calibrated to detect the Gamma frequencies.

- **BETA** (low-, mid- or high-range / 30-13 Hz) — Associated with mental alertness, hand-eye coordination, visual acuity, mild agitation, full attention, concentration, logical thinking, active conversation, cognition. You are relaxed at the lower frequencies, yet focused. Again, at the higher levels, stress hormones are released into the body. Beta training is helpful to those diagnosed with some types of Attention Deficit Disorder (ADD).

- **ALPHA** (13-8 Hz) — Associated with gentle relaxation, visualization, creative energy, expanded awareness, not agitated, tranquil, day-dreaming, not drowsy, semiconscious of time and space. At this level, healing chemicals are released into the body (those peptides, endorphins) which repair and heal the body. Alpha training can be helpful for dealing with stress.

- **THETA** (8-4 Hz) — Associated with meditation, intuition, inner peace and relaxation, super-learning, self-hypnosis, creativity, inspiration, dream recall, rapid eye movement (REM), recalling long-forgotten memories, heightened receptivity, fantasy, imagery, visions or hallucinations, memory, spirituality — overall, a very positive and expansive state.

- **DELTA** (4 and lower Hz) — Associated with detached awareness, unaware of time and space, deep dreamless non-REM sleep, trance, unconscious. Healing and regeneration of mind and body occur through the release of Human Growth Hormone (HGH) while in this state; this deep restorative sleep is essential to the healing process.

The frequencies of your brain waves affect how you feel, and how you respond to what's going on around you. While there can be external influences that affect the activity in your brain over which you have no control, you can control your brain wave levels, as well as your stress levels.

The chart below shows how your brain wave levels and stress levels are related — the lower (or slower) your brain waves frequencies are, the lower your stress levels will be:

Frequency (Hz)	Level of Mind / Stress
30 and above	High Stress
29–25	Mild Stress
24–20	Normal
19–14	Little Relaxed
13–11	Light Trance (Quiet Relaxed)
10–8	Moderate Trance (Very Relaxed)
7–5	Deep Trance (Deeply Relaxed)
4–2	Sleep
1	Unconscious
0.5	Coma
0	Death

The levels of your brain wave frequencies naturally will vary during the course of the day, mainly staying in the Beta and higher Alpha frequencies.

As you can see by taking a look at that chart, when you go to sleep, and throughout your sleep cycle, these frequencies will slow down all the way down to the Delta state. Normal sleep patterns will bring the activity up to the Alpha state, then back down into the Delta state; with this pattern occurring several times during your sleep cycle.

Meditation naturally lowers brain wave frequencies.

We intentionally lower our brain wave frequencies by using breathing to induce the Relaxation Response, coupled with visualization techniques in order to reach the Theta state. *You'll read more about the Relaxation Response in chapter 10.*

Feeling Floaty Or Numb?

During meditation, you may begin to feel numb, detached or tingly, or may even experience the sensation of floating. This is natural, and is caused by your brain waves slowing down.

As your brain wave frequencies slow down to the Theta state — either during meditation or during sleep cycles — neuro-transmitters, or chemical messengers, (glycine, and gamma-amino-butyric acid — or GABA) switch off specific cells in the brain that allow muscle movement causing what is commonly referred to as sleep paralysis, or pseudo paralysis.

That little twitch or "jerk" you may experience when you are falling asleep is an effect that can occur naturally during the transition of entering this state — a random electrical discharge (remember, your brain is an electrochemical organ).

A part of your brain essentially blocks the signals from your brain to your skeletal muscles — your brain is naturally paralyzing you to keep you from acting out your dreams.

When sleep paralysis doesn't occur, people may experience sleep walking.

Remember that your subconscious does not distinguish between what is real and what is not — when you are dreaming, your subconscious accepts your dreams as reality. If you were not "paralyzed," you would be physically acting out your dreams.

Imagine the possible harm that could occur if this block *didn't* happen and you were dreaming that you were chasing your cat out into the street.

The first time you experience this feeling during meditation may be a little uncomfortable, or even a little scary. Once you realize that it is natural, you will be able to relax, and you will accept that you have nothing to fear.

...Or Feeling High?

One of the benefits of practicing meditation is experiencing the release of the body's natural opiates — generically referred to as endorphins — which brings about more than just the lowering of stress levels.

Endorphins also reduce or relieve pain, boost the immune system, relax the body and mind, slow down the aging process, and lower blood pressure.

These endorphins that are created naturally by the body during meditation are safe and non-addictive with no negative side effects, and they produce a natural high!

STUDENT CHALLENGE!

If You Like to Do Your Own Research:

- In 1998, the healing benefits of prayer were alluded to when a group of scientists in the US studied how patients with heart conditions experienced fewer complications following periods of "intercessory prayer."

- Dr. Andrew Newberg, University of Pennsylvania, conducted studies using brain imaging to pinpoint areas of the brain involved when Franciscan nuns pray and Tibetan Buddhist monks meditate. Scientific study of both the physical world and the inner world of human experiences are, according to Dr. Newberg, equally beneficial. He commented that when someone has a mystical experience, they perceive that sense of reality to be far greater and far clearer than our usual everyday sense of reality. And, since the sense of spiritual reality is more powerful and clear, perhaps that sense of reality is more accurate than our scientific everyday sense of reality.

- At a meeting of the American Association for the Advancement of Science in Boston, scientists from Stanford University detailed their research into the positive effects that hypnotherapy can have in helping people cope with long-term illnesses.

THINK TIME:

What steps can you take to slow down your brain waves?

NOTES • THOUGHTS • IDEAS:

CHAPTER NINE

MEDITATION AND THE (TEENAGE) BRAIN

Meditation is the dissolution of thoughts in eternal awareness
or pure consciousness without objectification,
knowing without thinking, merging finitude in infinity.
— Voltaire, author

Teen Stress...

Teens are one of the two most highly-stressed age groups — the other highly-stressed group is the elderly. As a teen, you are at the awkward age between childhood and adulthood. You don't want to be treated like a child, but you also are not being treated like the adult you may think you are.

When you consider all the changes that you are going through during your teen years — with physical changes (puberty, hormones), emotional changes, and changes to your brain — it's no wonder you are stressed.

Reducing your stress is important to your mental health as well as your physical health. Many teens are fighting battles, conquering demons, trying to understand their emotions, and dealing with a multitude of issues on a day-to-day basis.

... And The Teenage Brain

The teenage brain differs from the adult brain. It processes information differently, and functions from a place of emotion rather than logic.

As a teenager, your brain is still under construction; it's not fully developed, and won't be until you are in your early- to mid-twenties. There is a lot going on with you physically during your teenage years, including brain development.

The physiological changes begin in the pre-teen years — at about 11 to 12 years of age — and this development continues throughout your teenage years and into your early twenties.

Changes To The Teen Brain Include These Areas:

- **The Frontal Cortex** — the rational part of the brain that recognizes new or foreign concepts, and determines the necessity to act; this process can be slower for teens who tend to just react.

- **The Amygdala** — a part of the limbic system, the emotional part of the brain associated with emotional responses; teens use this part more than the "thinking" part of their brain (the Frontal Cortex).

- **The Corpus Callosum** (cable of nerves connecting the two hemispheres) and the **Cerebellum** (the part associated with muscle coordination and movement, and the thinking process) also go through dynamic development during the teenage years.

Who's In Charge?

As a teen, the "CEO" of your brain is the limbic system, located beneath the cerebral cortex — an emotional part of the brain, and the seat of instinct.

When stress levels are high, a teen's concentration and memory can be affected which interferes with cognitive functioning.

This will have a domino effect and cause problems in many areas including school and relationships.

At your age, your responses to your world will tend to be based more on emotion than logic. Whether it is a verbal or a physical response, when something happens that provokes a response, yours will be an emotional one.

Here's an example:

Think of the last time you and a friend got into an argument. Very few of you would go to your friend and say, "You know, we really need to sit down and discuss this issue. We need to just have a cup of tea, and work out our problem."

More likely — you just had an emotional exchange, perhaps screaming at each other, calling each other names, smacking one another, shedding a few tears...

As you age into your early to mid-twenties, the frontal lobes kick in and the thinking process becomes more logical. At this stage of development, you actually *can* sit down and discuss your differences over a cup of tea.

No Excuses...

While this information is helpful to know as a teenager — you also need to recognize that this is *not* an *excuse* for bad behavior, but rather an *explanation* for your behavior.

You still are responsible for your actions — no matter your age or level of maturity.

Interesting Stuff You Just Might Like...

- During meditation, there may be an increase in activity in the front part of the brain, the area that is activated when one focuses their attention, as well as a decrease in activity in the back part of the brain, or parietal lobe, which is the area responsible for orientation, which suggests that meditation may lead to experiencing a loss of the sense of self, space and time.

- The brain is about $1/50^{th}$ of the body's weight, but uses about $1/20^{th}$ of its blood supply, and needs about $1/5^{th}$ of the body's oxygen and calories.

- According to research by Paul Ekman, University of California San Francisco Medical Center, meditation and mindfulness can calm the amygdala, the area of the brain responsible for fear memory.

THINK TIME:

Think about the last time you were upset with a friend, and how you reacted.

NOTES • THOUGHTS • IDEAS:

CHAPTER TEN

STRESS RESPONSE vs. RELAXATION RESPONSE

Feelings come and go like clouds in a windy sky.
Conscious breathing is my anchor.
– Thích Nhất Hạnh, Vietnamese Zen Monk

Physiology Of Stress...

We come into this world with natural instincts, the strongest of which is our instinct for survival — commonly referred to as the "fight or flight response," or as the "stress response."

When you find yourself in a situation that you perceive to be harmful, dangerous, or otherwise confrontational, your brain responds quickly and activates the "fight or flight response." The stress hormones — adrenaline and cortisol — flood your bloodstream to increase your body's metabolism and overcome the effects of fatigue to sustain your fight or flight, and to keep you alive.

This is a primal instinct.

There also is a third response to stress: "freeze."

There are some people who will not stand and fight, nor do they flee when faced with a threat. They don't know what to do or how to react. Fear overcomes them so severely, they freeze.

All of these responses elevate stress levels.

The Stress Response

The fact that the fight or flight response can produce high levels of stress can be a good thing when it is serving to keep you alive.

This stress response is vital to your survival when you perceive that you are in a dangerous or threatening situation.

When that stress response — or survival instinct — kicks in, a part of your brain known as the hypothalamic-pituitary-adrenal (HPA) system is activated.

Several hormones and catecholamines are released into your body, including adrenaline (epinephrine), dopamine, norepinephrine, and cortisol.

Your autonomic nervous system increases your heart rate by signaling it to pump harder, your digestive process slows down, blood pressure increases, breathing becomes more rapid, your lungs take in more oxygen, your blood supply is pulled to your body's core and away from your extremities, blood vessels in your skin and intestines are narrowed which increases blood flow to your major muscle groups, minor muscle control is diminished, and your body is prepared to fight the threat, or to run from it.

In a survival situation, this is all a good thing. However, prolonged or chronic stress is unhealthy.

Over a period of time, unchecked stress can take its toll on your body. When stress is not controlled, the body responds with physical ailments including high blood pressure, stomach or digestive problems, headaches and body aches, decreased immunity, and a multitude of other diseases. The effects of stress on the mind and body are covered in more detail in chapter 11.

Real Or Perceived?

This is a good time to point out that the threat only has to be *perceived* — it doesn't have to be a real threat for your stress levels to be elevated.

Remember that your subconscious does not distinguish between what is real and what is not; any threat that is perceived — real or not — will cause your body to go into the survival mode.

While We're Into Science Here: Let's Talk Nervous System!

Your nervous system is comprised of the central nervous system — or central processing unit (just like a computer) — which includes your brain and spinal cord, and the peripheral nervous system.

There are two components of the peripheral nervous system — the somatic nervous system (SONS) and the autonomic nervous systems (ANS). In simple terms, the SONS is the voluntary nervous system and the ANS is the involuntary nervous system.

The ANS consists of two divisions: the sympathetic nervous system (SNS) and the parasympathetic nervous system (PSNS).

So, What Does All *That* Have To Do With Stress?

There's a connection between your nervous system and its components to stress and relaxation.

The SNS is responsible for putting the body into the survival mode, or for inducing stress response; it makes demands on the body, calling for energy to burn immediately for fighting or fleeing. The PSNS, on the other hand, restores the calm; it is responsible for the relaxation response — PSNS slows the heart rate and breathing.

The Relaxation Response

Once a perceived threat or danger has passed, your body will naturally return to a relaxed state. Your heart rate, breathing, and blood flow eventually will return to normal.

To help things along, and to induce the relaxation response, you simply have to breathe. The relaxation response is the *opposite* of the stress response.

When you breathe in through your nose, air rushes past those nerve endings in your nasal passages and stimulates the calming centers of your brain. Opiates — your body's feel-good chemicals — are released into your body to help you to relax.

Have you ever been upset about something and had someone tell you, "Just take a breath!"? Try it!

The next time you are feeling a little stressed out, just breathe. In fact, try it now. Take a few deep breaths. Close your eyes, and just focus on your breathing for a minute or two.

You will feel your body begin to relax. You will be experiencing the relaxation response.

What can it do for you? It can lower your blood pressure and the levels of stress hormones, decrease pain and muscle tension, improve sleep and your energy levels, and so much more!

When practicing meditation, breathing is a key element to achieving relaxation, and reaching the Theta state.

Simply breathing can work any place, and any time that you need to reduce stress or just relax, and you don't have the time — or the situation is not conducive — for meditation.

Just breathe.

THINK TIME:

Can you feel the difference in your body
between stress and relaxation?

NOTES • THOUGHTS • IDEAS:

CAUSES and EFFECTS OF STRESS

For I will restore health unto thee,
and I will heal thee of thy wounds, saith the Lord;
because they called thee an Outcast, saying,
This is Zion, whom no man seeketh after.
— Jeremiah 30:17

What Causes You To Feel Stress?

Stress is a normal part of life. It can be a good thing when It pushes us to achieve, or puts us into survival mode.

Remember that our strongest instinct is the survival instinct or "stress response" which causes the "flight or fight" syndrome. However, too much stress — or unchecked stress — can wreak havoc with your nervous system, internal organs, etc. *(Didn't you just read about this in the last couple of chapters?)*

Consider the things in your life that cause you stress.

As a teen, your life is all about change, pressure, and STRESS! So much is going on in your life!

Let's think about all those things that can cause you stress. These might include:

- Parents, grandparents, guardians, siblings
  Are your parents always telling you what to do? Is your
  little brother or sister always bugging you?
- Boyfriends / girlfriends / best friends
- Death, divorce, or separation in the family
  Have you experienced the death of a family member,
  a close friend, or even a class mate? Are your parents
  always fighting, separated or getting a divorce?

- Parents get back together after divorce/separation

    *Are your parents trying to work it out, but still
    fighting? Putting you in the middle? Ignoring you?*

- Marriage or pregnancy/childbirth

    *Lots of planning and anticipation for either your
    marriage or pregnancy/childbirth, or someone else in
    your household? Someone unexpectedly pregnant?*

- Gaining a new family member

    *Grandparent move in? Got a new baby in the house?
    Maybe a new step-parent, or step-siblings?*

- Parents who are absent from the home

    *Living in a single-parent home? Or, a no-parent home?
    Living in foster care?*

- Parents travel a lot (without kids), such as for job

    *Almost as bad as a parent who is totally absent from
    the home is the one who is always gone for work and
    misses your recitals, plays, games, birthdays...*

- Incarceration or other court-ordered program

- A new job or responsibility (home or school)

    *A new job can cause some stress, no matter how much
    you might like what you do. Have you gained a new
    responsibility — have to take care of siblings after
    school? Have to do the laundry or cooking? Learning to
    drive?*

- Theft of personal possessions

    *So, you saved for months to buy your new phone —
    down-loaded music, took lots of pictures, have all your
    contacts in it — and someone ripped you off...*

- Illness or injury of self, family member, close friend

    *Think about training for a big game (football,
    basketball, etc.), and being in an accident that leaves*

you with a broken leg. This big game was going to be
your chance to shine, and now that opportunity is gone.
Think about your family member who has been in a
horrible accident that has left them with severe brain
damage and now you have to help take care of them.

- Attempting to break habits (*e.g.* eating, smoking, drinking)
  Try something as relatively easy as cutting sugar from
  your diet; all of a sudden, a nice cold soda sounds so
  good, or that cinnamon roll smells so amazing...

- Moving to a new community
  Parents moved the family out of state, and now you
  have to try to make new friends? Ever been the new kid
  at school?

- Change in health
  Something as common as a cold, or as serious being
  diagnosed with a chronic health condition — like cancer
  — can be stressful and send stress levels sky-rocketing.

- Change in financial status
  The economy can wreak havoc on a family. Dad
  gets laid off from his job, mom's babysitting job is
  dwindling, bills don't get paid, the electricity gets
  turned off, the car gets repossessed. Or, the opposite:
  suddenly coming into a lot of money also can cause
  stress — inheritance, lottery, etc. Now everyone is your
  best friend and seems to think they should get a cut!

- Job/Work (bosses, co-workers)
  Regardless of how much you like your job, there will be
  things you don't like about it, and people you don't like!

- Starting a new activity (*e.g.* extracurricular/school)
  First day of band or play practice, the day you start that
  new job, your first day in middle school or high school...

- SCHOOL (this is a biggie!)

    Teachers and staff, peers and classmates, academic
    difficulties, being bullied or threatened at school

- What else? _____

Good Stress vs. Bad Stress

Recognize that not all stressors are bad or traumatic; some stressors can be good things — like parents reuniting, an outstanding personal achievement, etc.

The good stress (or "eustress") these good things create can have as much of an impact on you as the bad stress (or "distress") created by the negative things that happen in your life.

For example, let's imagine that you are a "C" student, and you just get by in school. You are taking a class that you really like, and have a teacher who really connects with her students. For the first time ever, you get an "A" on your report card.

Now, because you have raised the bar, and you have shown that you are capable of higher grades, you are expected to perform at a higher level in all your classes.

Congratulations, you have just elevated your stress levels. The pressure is on to perform at this higher level.

HOMEWORK ASSIGNMENT!

So, determine how many of the things listed above are causing stress in your life, and make your own list. Think about how much stress each of the things on your list is causing you — does it bother you just a little bit, or does it bother you a lot?

Make a simple chart if it will help you to see where your stress levels are. Name each event using whatever labels you want, and assign a value from 1 to 10 to each event that causes you stress, with 1 being just a little, and 10 being a lot. This may help you to see what it is that is causing you the most stress in your life, and help you put it all into perspective.

Your chart may look something like this:

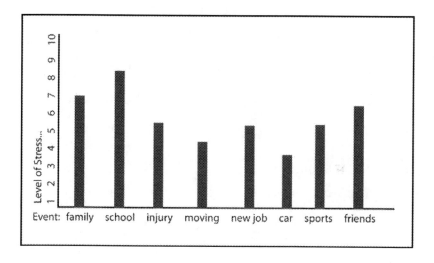

Think about all these things that are causing you stress, and take another look at your chart.

If you are highly stressed, you increase your chance of becoming ill, as your immune system is affected. Severe stress also presents a strong possibility that you will experience a significant change in behavior, feelings and/or physical well-being.

Do you have any control over what is causing your stress?

If not, learn to let it go — easier said than done. And learn to control what affect it has on you, and how you respond to it — again, easier said than done.

How else can you determine your stress levels?

You need to listen to your body.

How Does Your Body Respond To Stress?

As already mentioned, stress can have quite a negative effect on your health. It can take its toll on your brain and nervous system, skin, muscles, joints, heart, stomach, pancreas, intestines, reproductive system, and your immune system.

How do you know when you are experiencing high levels of stress?

Your body will give you numerous signals — whether physical, emotional, behavioral, or cognitive. Learn to recognize your body's signs of stress, which may include any of the following:

The Physical Signals
- Rapid heartbeat, pounding heart; even chest pain
- Feeling fatigued
- Headache, stomach ache
- Hard to breathe
- Queasiness, nausea, vomiting
- Sweating heavily
- Sweaty hands, cold hands
- Dizziness or blurred vision
- Dry mouth, hard to swallow
- Crave certain foods (women: carbs, men: meat)

The Emotional Signals
- Loss of emotional control
- Depression
- Intense anger or agitation
- Guilt, grief, denial
- Anxiety or fear
- Feeling overwhelmed

The Behavioral Signals

- Angry or emotional outbursts
- Hard to sleep
- Antisocial acts, withdrawal
- Diminished or increased appetite
- Suspiciousness
- Hyper awareness of surroundings
- Change in speech patterns

The Cognitive Signals

- Lack of concentration
- Confusion and lack of attention
- Loss of sense of time
- Poor decision-making
- Problems with abstract thinking, problem-solving
- Disturbing thoughts, nightmares

If you are experiencing any of these symptoms, go back and take a look at your stressors. And, recognize that you need to do something to reduce the stress in your life.

*In addition to meditation, this includes finding someone
you can trust to talk to about your problems,
which seems to be a tough thing for teens to do.*

I like using mental exercises with my students to help illustrate the importance of working together, and asking for help.

Some of the exercises we do in class require students to rely on each other for help. These always seem to be the most challenging for students. I encourage you to find some mental exercises, such as those as discussed in chapter 21, and see how much easier they are when you work with someone else to find the answers to the problems.

You Cannot Escape Stress

You have no control over most of what goes on around you, and what is causing the stress that surrounds you. You can, however, control how you react or respond to those environmental factors, and how you allow them to affect you.

This is where simple breathing exercises can help — and, of course, meditation — to calm and clear your mind.

Struggles are a part of life.

We all have challenges thrown at us, sometimes every day.

How you handle these struggles can make you stronger.

Have you ever faced a challenge with apprehension, then after accomplishing it, looked back and thought to yourself, "Well, that wasn't so hard!" or "Wow, I did that!"?

Always take time to think about what you have learned from any struggle or challenge you have had to face.

THINK TIME:

Do you recognize what is causing your stress?

Do you recognize your body's signals?

I am sharing the following story because students really like it, and they have asked that it be included in this book:

The Struggle of the Butterfly

A man found a cocoon of a butterfly.

One day a small opening appeared and he sat and watched the butterfly as it struggled for several hours to force its body through the little hole. Then it seemed to stop making any progress. It appeared it had gotten as far as it could.

The man decided to help the butterfly, so he took a pair of little scissors and snipped off the remaining bit of cocoon.

The butterfly then emerged easily, but it had a swollen body and small, shriveled wings.

The man continued to watch the butterfly because he expected that, at any moment, the wings would expand and be able to support the body, which would contract in time.

Neither happened! In fact, the butterfly spent its whole life crawling around with a swollen body and shriveled wings.

It was never able to fly.

What the man, in kindness and haste, did not understand was that the restricting cocoon and the struggle required to get through the tiny opening were God's way of forcing fluid from the body of the butterfly into its wings so that it would be ready for flight once it achieved freedom.

Sometimes struggles are exactly what we need in our life. If God allowed us to go through life without obstacles, it would cripple us. We would not be as strong as we could have been.

And — we would never fly.

– Author unknown

NOTES • THOUGHTS • IDEAS:

CHAPTER TWELVE

TAKE A BREATH — TRY TO SEE THE BIG PICTURE

I want to know how God created this world.
I am not interested in this or that phenomenon,
in the spectrum of this or that element.
I want to know His thoughts; the rest are details.
– Albert Einstein, physicist [3]

Have you ever been upset about something, and had someone tell you, "Just take a breath!"? *(Sound familiar?)*

So, take a breath! Feel better?

How long did that take? A second or two?

Can you spare a second or two out of your life if it will help you see things more clearly?

Teens tend to live in their own little black and white world of emotion, filled and fueled by their idealism.

Normal? Yes. Stressful? Yes.

Can you do anything about it? Yes.

Remember back in chapter nine — reading the explanation of your emotional responses? Remember that part about this all being an *explanation*, not an *excuse for bad behavior*?

Ultimately, you are responsible for your behavior, and your reactions; this "big picture" thing will help you get a grip on that.

There is a greater benefit to taking that breath when you are upset than just inducing the relaxation response. That moment it takes for you to take a breath may give you just enough time to get a glimpse of the "big picture" — the bigger story behind whatever it is that is upsetting you.

Seeing that big picture can be a bit of a challenge for teenagers — whose world is usually filled with extremes and emotions.

Again, let's go back to chapter nine — whether they are verbal or physical, your responses to your world at this age tend to be *emotional*, and this is what makes it difficult for you to see the big picture.

We all see our own little part of the big picture, but none of us can truly see the *whole* picture. There is way too much to try to see or understand — the world is far too complex.

Our vision of the world is generally based on our personal perspective — drawn from our personal life experiences, and our personal backgrounds or upbringing.

Here's an exercise that you can do that will help to explain:

Make a little circle with your hand by curling your hand and touching the tip of your index finger to the tip of your thumb. You've just made a make-believe viewer of the world!

Now, hold your hand up to your eye and look through the center of that circle.

Pick one area in the room to focus on, and try to come up with a story based on what you see through your little make-believe viewer. Try to get every detail you can of this little picture, and write a story of life in this room based *only* on what you see through your little make-believe viewer.

Are you able to tell a story of life in this room? Is your story accurate, based on what you see?

Does *your* story tell the *whole* story of life in this room, or just a part of it?

What if 20 students were in the same room with you, doing this same exercise, and writing their own stories of life in this room — based on what they see through their little make-believe viewers?

Now, what if we were to put all of those stories together — would *that* tell the *whole* story of life in this room?

Even if there were 50 or 100 students all in the same room, doing the same exercise, writing their little stories based on what they see, then combining all of those stories of life in this room into one big story, these stories *still* would not tell the *whole* story — or show the big picture — of life in this room.

Now imagine trying to tell the story of life in the whole house or building, or the block you live on, or the city you live in, or the state, or the country where you live.

Think about this for just a minute: this country where you live is just one of many on this planet, and this planet is just one of many in our solar system, which is part of one of many galaxies, which is part of one of many universes. *Whew!*

Let's put this a different way: you know how tiny a grain of sand is. Consider that you are like a grain of sand living in a house, that is like a grain of sand on a planet, that is like a grain of sand in a galaxy, that is like a grain of sand in a universe...

What if this exercise represented the story of all of our lives, not just the story of life in this room?

Is that whole "big picture" thing coming into focus now?

When you find yourself in a situation where you are allowing someone or something to upset you — pause a moment. Don't react. Take a breath.

Give yourself those few seconds or so that it takes to take a few breaths. Allow your brain to sort out what it is that is happening and what it is that is getting you upset.

Take another breath, then another, and another. Try counting to 10. Keep doing this until you feel yourself becoming calmer, and then respond to whatever it is that is upsetting you.

Learn To Change Your Perspective

You also can try to change your perspective to help you to see that big picture.

If someone is annoying you, try to see the situation from *their* perspective — from *their* point of view.

There is an old proverb about not passing judgment on someone until you have walked a mile in their shoes. By placing yourself in their "shoes," you may be able to understand their perspective. Remember that each of our points of view is based on our individual life experiences. What might that person's experiences include?

Even if you don't understand that person's actions or choices, or their life experiences, by taking that moment to take a breath, you still can make an effort to see through their eyes.

For what it's worth, this is where our faith can come into play, too. While we only see a small part of that big picture, we need to have faith that God sees the big picture. He not only knows the whole story; He wrote the book and He knows how it ends.

THINK TIME:

What steps can you take to see the big picture?

NOTES • THOUGHTS • IDEAS:

CHAPTER THIRTEEN

EQUIP YOURSELF WITH HEALTHY TOOLS!

You cannot teach a man anything;
you can only help him to find it within himself.
– Galileo, scientist / astronomer

What Can You Do To Reduce Stress?

Once you have identified the causes and symptoms of stress, you need to learn a few ways you can reduce that stress in safe, healthy and natural ways — an important element in maintaining a healthy body and a healthy mind.

First: BREATHE!

Now, take a look at your perspective of your life.

Here's an oldie, but goodie: fill a glass with water to the halfway point. When you look at this glass of water, do you see your glass as half full or half empty?

If you see your glass as half empty, you are someone who tends to view your world more on the negative side; if the glass is half full, you tend to see things in a more positive light.

Always Try To Be Positive!

Studies have shown that thinking *positive* thoughts and using *positive* visualization will release endorphins into your system and make you feel better — mentally and physically.

Think about this: a placebo is something with no pharmacological effect that is given to a patient who believes they are receiving the real thing. Placebos work because the *positive* mind set causes the release of the endorphins, which eases the pain.

The key word here: positive.

One way to focus on the positive is to count your blessings — a lesson I learned from my mother. Even though she had a difficult childhood, she always found something she could be thankful for.

Ask yourself these five questions she once asked me:

Did you eat today?

A lot of people did not. If you did, and your tummy is full more often than not, you are blessed.

Do you have a roof over your head?

A lot of people do not. If you have shelter from the weather, and a place to lay your head at night, you are blessed.

Are there people in your life who love you?

There are many people who go through their day feeling unloved and unwanted. If there are people who love you no matter what you do, you are blessed.

Is there someone in your life you love?

There are people who have no one to love. If you can share your life with someone, and feel love for them, you are blessed.

Do you live in a country where — for the most part — you are free to express yourself?

There are countries where a person can lose his life for saying something the government finds offensive. If your answer to this question is yes, you are blessed.

Again, Count Your Blessings!

Be positive — see your glass as half full.

Stay focused on the good stuff!

Instead of focusing on what you don't have, stay focused on — and show gratitude for — what you do have in your life.

Make a list of all of your blessings — those things you have to be grateful for every day!

Tape this list to your mirror, and look at it every day to remind yourself that there are things in your life that you can count as blessings.

What Else?

There are lots of other ways to reduce the stress in your life.

Meditation is, of course, a wonderful way to reduce stress and one that I highly recommend. It is a powerful tool that you can use almost any time or any place.

However, there may be times when meditation isn't practical. It's a good idea to create and keep handy a list of alternative methods you can use to reduce your stress.

A simple way to come up with these alternative methods you can use is to create a list of safe, healthy and natural ways to reduce or control your stress — things that you know will work for *you* — any time or any place.

This list can be any activity you could do (write, draw, play, work out or exercise, etc.), something you could eat (ah, comfort food!), or some place you could go (physically or mentally).

HOMEWORK ASSIGNMENT!

Take out a piece of paper (maybe you could use the back of the paper with the list of your blessings) and list the alphabet from A to Z (refer to the sample list below) leaving room next to each letter to write the things that you want on your list. Then, start your list of things you can do to reduce your stress.

Make it personal — list YOUR favorite things.

Be creative. When you have finished, you will have a list of options that will work for you. Keep this list some place handy. Then, the next time you are feeling stressed, mentally go through the alphabet and think about all those things on your list. Keep going until you hit on something that will work — right then and there — to lower your stress.

A few ideas to get you started are on the sample list below. You can use this list to help to get you started, but you should create your own list, using your own ideas — things you know will work for *you*.

A = Apple; Aerobics; Ask for help; Adventure

B = Blessings; Breathe; Baseball; Basketball; Banana

C = Chocolate; Cry; Call a friend; Calm yourself; Camp

D = Dance; Drive; Dive into water; Draw; Do something fun

E = Eat healthy food; Exercise; Examine your life

F = Friends; Family; Fishing; Find joy; Find a quiet place

G = God (pray); Game; Gardening; Grandparents

H = Help someone; Humor; Happy place; Have fun

I = Ice cream; Imagine; Instrument *(play / learn to play)*

J = Journal; Jog; Joke; Join a club or group

K = Kickball; Kite; Kindness; Kiss someone you love

L = Laugh; Let go *(even for a little while)*; Laps *(track or pool)*

M = **MEDITATE**; Music; Make something; Motivate

N = Nap; "No"; Nature; Novel *(read or write one)*; Nutrition

O = Organize; Outdoors; Orange juice

P = Pray; Pamper; Play; Peace; Positive thoughts

Q = Quiet place; Quit harmful habits

R = Run; Read; Rest; Relaxation exercise

S = Sing; Swim; Smile; Sports; Spirituality

T = Thanks; Talk; Tai Chi; Take a walk; Tea (herbal)

U = Unite with friends; Use your brain (puzzles)

V = Volunteer; Vacation; Visualization

W = Walk; Write; Work out; Warm and cozy place

X = "X"ercise; Xylophone *(play one!)*

Y = Yoga; Yell (release); Yawn; "Yes" to life

Z = Zoo; Zen; Zero out your day

Sit down and take some time to make the list your own, and keep adding to it when you think of something new.

More Body Chemistry...

Do you remember what you read in previous chapters about the opiates in your body?

When you think about your life in a positive way, your body creates opiates that elevate your mood. Opiates — endorphins — are the neurotransmitters that reduce pain.

There are several ways to get your body to produce these opiates, such as meditation (of course), working out (ask a runner about a "runner's high") eating chocolate, laughing, or just with a little exposure to ultraviolet (UV) light by going out and getting some sun.

Acupuncture and acupressure also will produce this effect.

Experiencing something special through your senses of sight, smell, hearing, and touch also can elevate your mood, such as *seeing* something you perceive as beautiful, or *watching* a movie that you find enjoyable, or *listening* to beautiful music.

Who doesn't feel better when you *smell* a freshly-baked batch of cookies! And think about the *feeling* of snuggling under a soft, warm blanket on a cold night!

These are just a few examples of ways to reduce your stress, and to work on your healthy body and healthy mind. Now, take some time to sit down and think of some things that will work for *you*.

STUDENT CHALLENGE:

I am going to guess that I am not the only one who enjoys doing research — I challenge you to do a little extra research on your own to learn more about your body and how it works.

THINK TIME:

Make that list of what you can use to reduce your stress,
and count your blessings!

NOTES • THOUGHTS • IDEAS:

NOTES • THOUGHTS • IDEAS:

THE MIND-BODY CONNECTION TO MUSIC

Music hath charms to soothe the savage breast,
To soften rocks, or bend a knotted oak.
– William Congreve, author

The majority of my classes begin with a volunteer selecting a CD from an assortment I bring to class. These CDs consist of flute or acoustic guitar, classical music, ocean or nature sounds, or any of the other relaxing and meditative options I may have on hand.

The selection of music is important because it sets the tone for the class. Or, as one of my students once said, "It creates a nice backdrop for the class."

Music can be such a powerful tool for lowering stress, or for getting into a meditative state.

Why? Because the body and the brain resonate with the frequencies around them.

OK, so, what does *that* mean?

Think about the role of a cheerleader. Ask any athlete what happens when the cheerleaders get the crowd all pumped up and the crowd begins yelling and screaming at them. The team gets charged up with that energy. The athletes' bodies and brains are resonating with those frequencies.

Now consider a soft, soothing melody playing in the background while you are reading, doing homework, or just resting. You begin to relax.

The effect this gentle, soothing sound has on your body and brain is going to be quite different from the effect the sounds of the screaming crowd has on the athlete.

Another example: you go to a school dance or other activity where everyone is dancing wildly to loud, pounding music. Movements are frenetic, arms are waving, and bodies are bouncing all over the place.

You may have been calm and relaxed when you first walked into the room, but soon you begin to feel the excitement, too.

Your body and brain are resonating with the frequencies in the room.

Effects Of Music And Sound On The Brain

Rhythmic sounds produce a vibration which has a profound effect on the activity in our brains.

Many cultures use chanting, drums, gongs, chimes, and other instruments to create meditative sounds.

While studying the Shamanic State of Consciousness, a researcher named Melinda Maxfield discovered that the rhythmic beat of a drum struck 4.5 times per second was the key to transporting a shaman into the deepest part of his shamanic state of consciousness. That 4.5 beats — or cycles — per second correspond to the Theta state of brain wave activity, which is the most conducive to meditation.

Sound is measured in cycles per second (cps) or hertz (Hz). The average range of hearing for the human ear is between 16 Hz and 20,000 Hz. While we cannot hear extremely low frequencies (ELFs), we can perceive them as rhythm.

Researchers have studied neuro-acoustics and have produced music or sound CDs to aid in achieving specific states of brain wave activity, such as the Theta state.

NOTE: You should use caution when you subject yourself to any outside source which attempts to alter your brain in any way! This includes music.

Music can cause the release of those feel-good endorphins into your body — which will make you feel good *if* you select a type of music that is soothing.

The type of music you listen to is certainly going to have an effect on you. Your body and brain resonate with the frequencies around you. *(Remember reading that?)*

Selecting Music For Relaxation — An Experiment

When my son was in junior high back in the late 1980s, he conducted an experiment as a science fair project to determine the effects of music on plants.

He purchased five plants of the same size and variety, and put them on a shelf in his room.

Every day, he would place headphones on the pot of each of four plants and play a different type of music for each, keeping the fifth plant as a control (meaning it didn't get to "listen" to any music.)

He played an assortment of classical, country, classic rock, and heavy metal for the four plants — exposing each to its assigned music for about five minutes, twice a day, over a period of about three weeks.

He documented his observations each day.

Because I love classical music, I had hoped that the classical music plant would flourish. Wrong. The classical was the smallest and "droopiest" at the end of the experiment; the heavy metal was the firmest and most wild-looking.

In retrospect, it all made sense. The softer frequencies "softened" and relaxed the classical plant; however, harsher frequencies "hardened" the heavy metal plant.

And So It Is With Our Bodies And Our Minds

When you expose yourself to loud, harsh sounds and a high energy environment, you will feel more stressed than when you expose yourself to smoother, softer, more relaxing sounds in a calmer environment.

When you are stressed and looking for a little relaxation, you need to surround yourself with softness — including the music you choose to play.

When you are preparing to get into a relaxed or meditative state, consider your surroundings. Find a quiet place where there will be no interruptions or distractions. And, play some appropriate music to help you relax.

What Difference Will It Make?

I had a student who shared with me that he used to listen to a lot of loud, harsh rap music. It's what he liked, and it's what his friends liked.

He noticed that he was always angry, had a "short fuse" and was getting into a lot of fights.

He had been in one of my classes when we discussed the impact music has on us; how we resonate with the frequencies around us.

Following that class, he said he started rethinking his choice of music; he made the decision to start listening to other types of music instead, including a Christian music radio station known for its positive and encouraging music. He got into the Christian music and listened to it more than any other type.

Within a few weeks of this decision, he had noticed a change in how he felt, and he told me that he found he was reacting differently to things. He wasn't angry all the time, and hadn't been getting into any fights.

The last time we spoke, he said he felt calmer, and that he smiled more now.

I smiled, too...

STUDENT CHALLENGE!

If you are interested in learning about earth frequencies, research the Schuman Resonance — the resonant frequency of the earth's electromagnetic field.

You also might want to do some research on the sounds of outer space.

THINK TIME:

Think about the types of music you listen to,
and the effects of that music on your body and brain.

NOTES • THOUGHTS • IDEAS:

CHAPTER FIFTEEN

VISUALIZATION / SETTING GOALS / ACHIEVEMENT OF GOALS

All our knowledge has its origins in our perceptions.

– Leonardo da Vinci, renaissance artist and painter

I often mention that I don't make resolutions; I prefer to set goals for myself.

And, I use meditation to help me achieve my goals.

When I meditate, I get a clear mental image of me achieving whatever the goal happens to be that I am focused on achieving. It doesn't matter how big or how small the goal is, by using visualization techniques, I am more likely to achieve that goal.

I encourage *you* to set goals for *yourself.*

The goals don't have to be complex or challenging. They can be as simple as eating all your vegetables for a whole week, or reading one book a month.

Remember that your subconscious mind does not distinguish between what is real and what is not; because of this, you can visualize yourself succeeding at those goals you have set, and your subconscious will lead you to that success.

How Does This Work?

Think about something that you want to accomplish in the next five minutes. What *exactly* do you want to have achieved in that short amount of time?

Take a few deep breaths, let yourself relax a little. Now, get a clear mental image of whatever that five-minute goal happens to be, and see yourself achieving it — to perfection.

Let's expand on this idea.

What goal would you like to set for the next hour — what do you want to have achieved in that amount of time?

How about the next 24 hours? Take a look at the clock. What do you want to have accomplished at this time tomorrow?

How about the next week? What day is today? What goal can you set that you can achieve by the same day next week?

How about the next month? The next three months?

Six months from now?

The hard one for most teens: what do you want to accomplish in the next year?

When I do this exercise with a class and have them write out their goals, this is the point in class when some students will drop their pencils on the desk. They just can't see a year ahead in their lives.

Even though it can be challenging to look a whole year into the future, think about what you might want to have achieved in that amount of time.

Now, Make A List!

5-minute goal:
1-hour goal:
24-hour goal:
1-week goal:
1-month goal:
3-month goal:
6-month goal:
1-year goal:
"some-day" goal:

Don't hesitate to set a few "some-day" goals, too! These are the things that you want to do *some day*, and can be as far-reaching as you want! *(FYI — my "some-day" goal: I want to visit outer space.)*

The process is the same — whether you are setting a small goal, or a big goal. You take a few deep breaths, relax a little, and get a clear mental image of whatever your goal happens to be.

If it helps, use holidays, or seasons or other significant dates as your goal dates — a birthday, for instance, or the first day of spring, or the last day of school.

Always see yourself achieving your goal — to perfection.

You may or may not see results right away; however, you will see results. You have planted the seed for success. Just like planting a garden, it sometimes takes a while for things to grow.

Be patient, and keep thinking about your goals and visualize yourself achieving them every day.

What If You Don't Achieve Your Goals?

It's a good idea to set deadlines for your goals, but when you don't quite achieve a goal by the deadline you have set for achieving that goal, don't think of it as a failure.

Instead, re-evaluate your plan — what worked, what didn't work — then make changes to your plan, and re-set the goal.

Think of it like this: let's say you set a goal to read three books in the next six weeks. You only get through the first two.

Re-evaluate.

Why were you unable to achieve your goal? Were the books not interesting enough to hold your attention? Do you need to spend more time reading each day? Do you need to allow more time to read each book in order to achieve this goal?

Now, adjust the plan and reset the goal.

Perhaps you set a new goal to read three books in the next eight weeks.

Sometimes you learn what doesn't work for you. Remember, that's a type of success, too.

Coming up in chapter 19, you will get a different perspective of mistakes and "happy accidents" — take your time reading that chapter, and think about that perspective.

Tips To Help You Achieve Your Goals

- Make lists of your goals, and set reasonable timelines for achieving them.
- Visualize how you will achieve your goal, and see yourself achieving it — always to perfection!
- Re-evaluate and edit your lists whenever *you* think it's necessary to help you achieve your goals.
- Tell people you trust about your goals to increase your probability of achieving them.

THINK TIME:

What are the goals you set for yourself for today?

NOTES • THOUGHTS • IDEAS:

NOTES • THOUGHTS • IDEAS:

CHAPTER SIXTEEN

MEDITATION TO IMPROVE SPORTS PERFORMANCE

Men go abroad to wonder at the heights of mountains,
at huge waves of the sea, at the long courses of the rivers,
at the vast compass of the ocean, at the circular motions of
the stars; and they pass by themselves without wondering.

– St. Augustine

Your body will believe what your brain tells it.

I have worked with various athletes over the years, and had some wonderful success stories. One student achieved a personal best record, one broke a school record, one set a state record, one swimmer "got her butt out of the water," and one, a body-builder, reached a goal he had been working to achieve for months.

Have you ever watched a sporting event — like the Olympics — and seen an athlete standing relatively motionless, with his or her eyes closed, perhaps moving their head and swaying a little?

They are visualizing their performance — and seeing themselves winning. They will see themselves running the race, going through their gymnastics routine, feeling the long jump — all in their head.

Their bodies will believe what their brains have told them.

Many coaches and athletes believe that using relaxation, visualization and even meditation will enhance physical performance. By using mental training — or mental rehearsal — athletes are able to visualize themselves performing their feats to perfection. As a result of this practice of visualization, they set themselves up for victory.

Whatever your sport happens to be, start visualizing yourself doing it — to perfection.

Let's say you are a baseball player. It's cold and snowy outside, so you can't go out and practice hitting the ball with your friends.

Instead, practice in your head.

Get into a relaxed, meditative state and play ball!

Visualize yourself standing in the perfect batting position at the plate with a bat in your hands. Feel the muscles in every part of your body that would be tensed to lift the bat back over your shoulder, and crouch over the plate. You know how this should feel to your body.

Now see the ball coming toward you, and visualize swinging the bat with all your strength and connecting with the ball, sending it sailing over the fence in left field.

Physically, you haven't moved or actually done any of this, but your subconscious mind believes you have.

The more you practice the visualization exercises, the better you will be when you are able to get out on the field and stand at the plate with the bat in your hands.

True Story:

I have worked with groups of students who had to run 1.5 miles in less than 12 minutes. It took six laps around the track to accomplish the distance that was required.

I would guide these students to get them into a relaxed state, then I would have them visualize themselves on the track. I would have them drop their arms to their sides, bend their elbows, and put their feet flat on the floor.

I then would have them imagine they were in the start position, and would tell them to visualize the start of the run.

I then would lead them through the first lap, telling them to see the first turn ahead, then the second, then the back stretch, then the third turn, then the fourth, then the home stretch. Keeping an eye on the clock, I would "pace" them at two minutes per lap, and would tell them to "feel" the run in their bodies — *to feel their legs stretch out ahead of them and their feet grab the track, to feel the air filling their lungs as they started breathing more heavily and rapidly, to feel their arms pumping with the rhythm of their legs* — but not to actually move any of the muscles in their bodies.

Because the subconscious doesn't distinguish between what's real and what's not (have you heard that before?), the students believed they had just run 1.5 miles.

At the end of their "run," some were out of breath, and some had to stand up to "shake it off."

I encouraged these students to have someone help them with the time-keeping and number of laps, and to practice this exercise as often as they could.

On test day, the majority of the students passed their test. There was one young man who had been concerned about the run who came over after he passed, gave me a hug, and thanked me for helping him make it.

Because he had practiced mentally, had conditioned his mind and body, and because he *believed* he could make it, he did.

THINK TIME:

> *Imagine you are playing your favorite sport*
> *and go through the motions — practice in your head.*

NOTES • THOUGHTS • IDEAS:

CHAPTER SEVENTEEN

USING MEDITATION TO TAP INTO CREATIVITY

The intuitive mind is a sacred gift and
the rational mind is a faithful servant.
We have created a society that honors the servant
and has forgotten the gift.

– Unknown

This whole program of mine started all because some graphic arts students asked me about creativity, where it comes from, and how to develop it.

My answer was, "Use meditation."

Go back to chapter eight and revisit the brain wave frequencies — go to the section that explains the Theta frequencies.

You will see that this state is associated with — among other things — *meditation, intuition, creativity, inspiration, heightened receptivity, fantasy, imagery, visions or hallucinations, memory...*

The Theta state is overall a very positive — and the most creative — state that is reached when you slow your brain waves down to between 4 to 8 Hz — or cycles per second.

And how, you might ask, does one do this?

Through meditation, of course!

You also reach this level when you sleep — this is the dream state, or REM state.

If you are already practicing meditation, you may be aware that sometimes it feels like you are dreaming.

At this stage, the noise of the conscious mind is quieted, so the creativity of the subconscious mind is free to create.

For those of you who are artistic on any level — whether you draw, paint, sketch, write poetry, stories, music or lyrics, play an instrument, sing, or dance — I recommend that you keep a pencil and paper next to your bed.

When you are first waking up in the morning and already in a relaxed state, you may be aware that some wonderful ideas are running through your head. It may be the perfect chord, an image of something you want to create, an idea for a short story, a song lyric, etc.

Don't wait until you are fully awake and out of bed — *write it down*. Don't worry about trying to make sense of it, *write it down*. Don't worry about spelling, or sentence structure, *write it down*.

You can sort it all out later.

Creativity On Demand

You can "program" yourself to think of something specific.

More times than I could count, I would look over the specs for a job I had been commissioned to do — the objective of the company, the target demographic, the preferences of the client, and so on — and I would sit quietly, drift into a meditative state, and go through these details in my mind. Then, I would just wait.

Before long, I would be writing or sketching out ideas on the note pad (meaning a pad of paper, not the electronic version) in my lap.

When you want to create something, write down as many details as you can about what it is you want to create.

For example: you want to create a poster for the wall in your room. Begin by writing down ideas for what you want the poster to include. Will it be just words or pictures? Realistic or abstract? Specific colors or shapes?

Be as specific as you can with the direction you want to go with this poster.

Read through your notes a few times. Next, get your note pad and pencil, and sit in a comfortable chair (or on the floor), and let yourself relax.

Breathe. Focus on your breath.

As you begin to find yourself in a relaxed state, begin to review the notes you wrote about your project.

As thoughts begin to pop into your head, write them down. If it's an image, sketch it out.

Again, don't worry about perfection at this stage; just get it down on paper. Don't try to make sense of it now — just write it all down.

When the ideas or images stop, look over what you have written down or sketched out, and begin to sort it out.

By staying in a relaxed state, the sorting out part will go more smoothly than if you try to force it.

Before you know it, you will have the idea for your poster!

This also will work for students who have to be creative for a science project, English composition paper, or art project, but who may not be creative by nature.

Use the same process of planning what you need to work on, writing all the details down, then getting into a relaxed or meditative state, and let the creativity flow.

I like to share a story about Thomas Edison with my students, about how he came up with some of his ideas for new inventions. He would sit in a chair and place metal plates (like pie tins) on the floor, on each side of the chair. He then would hold ball bearings in his hands, and let his arms hang down at his sides, with his hands positioned just above the metal plates.

As he relaxed and started to fall asleep (going from the Alpha state into the Theta state) he would reach what is known as the hypnagogic state — or stage 1 of the sleep cycle — the precise point where one transitions from wakefulness to sleep.

At this point, his hands would relax, he would drop the ball bearings, they would hit the metal plates, and he would awaken.

More often than not, he would have an answer to a problem, or a new idea, or inspiration for a new invention, or a method of solving a conundrum that had him perplexed.

Clearly, this was an effective tool for him to use — Edison was one of the world's most prolific inventors.

Meditation is a wonderful tool for *any* artistic soul — not only for the creative process, which is released in a meditative state, but also because the artistic soul may find it easier to achieve a state of meditation.

Students who are creative by nature will find it easier to get into a meditative state much easier than others — and find meditation to be quite beneficial to their creative process.

THINK TIME:
> *How will you use meditation to expand your creativity?*

NOTES • THOUGHTS • IDEAS:

NOTES • THOUGHTS • IDEAS:

CHAPTER EIGHTEEN

HOW HAVE YOU BEEN PROGRAMMED TO THINK?

There are two ways to live your life:
One is as though nothing is a miracle.
The other is as though everything is a miracle.

– Unknown

What do you suppose will happen if you wake up in the morning, look into the mirror, and say to yourself, "You are such a loser! This is going to be such a crappy day!"?

Chances are, you will feel like a loser all day, and will probably have a bad day.

Why? Because more often than not, you tend to get out of life what you expect to get out of life.

Now, rewind.

What might happen if you wake up in the morning, look into the mirror, and say to yourself, "You rock! This is going to be a great day!"?

Yep, chances are, you will feel good and have a good day.

Again, you tend to get out of life what you expect to get out of life.

Did you ever hear these types of comments when you were younger?

You can't do that!   *You won't!*
You're useless!   *You're wrong!*
You'll fail if you try!   *You can't win!*
What is wrong with you?   *You're such a dummy!*
You'll never amount to anything!

Because your subconscious accepts what is fed into it as real, you were conditioned to believe these comments were true.

Or — did you grow up hearing these types of comments?

Yes, you can do that!   *You are awesome!*

You can succeed at this!   *Yes, you can win!*

I am so proud of you!   *You are a wonderful kid!*

You can do anything if you put your mind to it!

Because your subconscious accepts what is fed into it as reality, you were conditioned to believe *these* comments were true.

Either way, your reality is based on how you have been programmed to think.

> *Whether you think you will have a good day*
> *or you think you will have a bad day — you are right.*

Where Do You Focus Your Attention?

Think about where you focus most of your attention.

Make a list of the things you did today. Be honest with yourself — which one did you talk about the most? Which bothered you the most, or stuck with you the most?

The majority of people focus their attention on the small part of the day that was bad, instead of the majority of the day that was good.

I asked a student to write out a list of things that happened during her day. Here is what her list included:

Woke up

Took a shower, brushed teeth, etc.

Fixed breakfast, ate breakfast

Took vitamins

Read and answered e-mails, and checked other messages

Put grocery list together

Got in car and drove to store

Some guy cut me off on the freeway!

Went into store, bought groceries

Took groceries home and put them away

Fixed lunch, ate lunch

Threw in some laundry

Checked e-mails and messages again

Decided what to fix for dinner

Phone calls with friends

Fixed dinner, ate dinner

Loaded the dishwasher

Watched TV for a while

Went to bed

I then asked her, "Of all the things that happened today, which did you talk about the most through e-mails, messages, texting, phone calls, etc.?"

Take a guess which one she talked about the most.

Yep — that guy who cut her off on the freeway.

Of the more than 20 things she had listed, the one she had focused on was the one bad thing that had happened all day — the one thing that had upset her the most.

I challenged her — and I challenge you — to start focusing your attention on the positive things, the good things, the things that go well in your life. Be more focused on your blessings instead of the problems in your life.

Sure, the bad things will still happen, but by changing your focus, you change the outcome and how you feel at the end of your day.

The more you program yourself to focus on the positive, the more you will notice the positive, and you will find yourself paying less attention to the negative.

And, the negative will affect you less.

Tomorrow morning, when you wake up, look into the mirror, and tell yourself: "You rock! This is going to be a great day!"

THINK TIME:

What steps can you take to change
your internal programming?

NOTES • THOUGHTS • IDEAS:

CHAPTER NINETEEN

A DIFFERENT PERSPECTIVE OF "MISTAKES"

No snowflake ever falls in the wrong place.
– Zen Saying

Ever make a mistake? Ever feel that you have failed at something? Ever make a fool of yourself in front of *everyone*?

Happy news! You're in good company!

A phrase I have come to use — especially when teaching at-risk students — is "we all fail forward."

If we are a little wise (and a little lucky), we learn from our "mistakes." I tell my students to look at the mistakes — or unwise decisions — as a learning experience. Even when you make an unwise decision, you still have learned *something*.

Sometimes we learn what doesn't work.

There is a story I like to share about Thomas Edison, the inventor. Apparently, he had been trying to find a material he could use as a filament for a light bulb. After thousands of attempts to find this material, and not being successful, Edison did not consider himself to be a failure. Instead, he considered himself to be the world's foremost expert on what would not work as a filament in a light bulb.

There are hundreds of stories about people who have been unsuccessful time after time, but because they did not give up, they eventually found success at whatever their chosen field happened to be.

In addition to the story about Edison, here are a few favorite stories (or so my students tell me) that I like to share about people who did not accept failure:

- Michael Jordan became a member of the varsity basketball team when he was in the 9th grade; then was cut from the team in the 10th grade.

- Henry Ford, J.C. Penney, and Walt Disney all had to file bankruptcy at some point in their lives, as did the very successful businessman and multi-billionaire, Donald Trump.

- Albert Einstein didn't speak until he was three or four years old, and throughout his school years, his teachers thought he was unintelligent and insubordinate — commenting on occasion that he would never amount to anything.

- Winston Churchill was defeated in an election after 22 years of serving in Parliament. He eventually came back to the political arena and went on to become Prime Minister of Great Britain.

Happy Accidents!

And then there are those things that are referred to as "happy accidents" — the things that turned out to be good things, even though they started out as mistakes or errors.

- Most people are familiar with the name Levi Strauss. Did you know he moved from New York to California way back in the 1850s with the intention of selling tents to Gold Rush prospectors? He had all this heavy, durable material with him to make the tents, but the miners didn't need tents. They needed trousers. So, Strauss came up with what we know today as Levi jeans!

- Back in the 1960s, some scientists at 3M Company came up with a type of glue that would stick pieces of paper together, but the sheets came apart easily. They thought the glue was worthless. Then an employee came up with the idea of using the glue to make bookmarks. Thus, the *Post-It* note was created.

- Right around that same time, scientists were trying to create an artificial rubber. Their happy accident is known as *Silly Putty.*
- Too many to list them all, there are countless other examples, including some medical discoveries — such as penicillin and x-rays — that were made when scientists were looking for something else.

Perhaps it's time you changed how you think about failure. When you are not successful at something, don't beat yourself up. Take a few minutes to re-evaluate what you did, what went wrong, and think about what you can do differently next time.

Take the time to step back, take a breath, look at the experience, and ask yourself, "What did I learn from this experience?"

Tell yourself, too, that *failure* doesn't have to mean you have failed at something — it can mean you just have learned something that doesn't work for you.

THINK TIME:

How can you turn a poor choice you have made
into a positive thing?

NOTES • THOUGHTS • IDEAS:

CREATING A FRESH START...

Therefore if any man be in Christ, he is a new creature:
old things are passed away;
behold, all things are become new.
– 2 Corinthians 5:17

Back in chapter 15 — the one on setting goals — I mentioned that I have never been one to make New Year's resolutions — mainly because I have never been good at keeping them.

I also mentioned that I do, however, set goals for myself — both short-term and long-term goals — and I find that I am more likely to achieve these.

This chapter will actually tie in really well with that chapter on setting goals. Go back and review it!

There is a saying that you can't move forward into your future until you let go of your past.

Learn to let go.

If you are standing there holding onto the door knob, you will need to let go of it before you can move through the doorway!

Take that leap of faith that will help move you forward toward achieving your goals. I understand that letting go and leaving the past in the past isn't that easy, is it?

However, until you do let go, the past will hold you back from achieving all you want to achieve in your future.

If you have a goal you want to achieve, take a look at what (or who) might hold you back from reaching it.

Think of it this way: you cannot change anything that already has happened. Anything you have said, anything you have done — it's all history now. Remember the good stuff and any lessons you have learned, and let go of the rest. Learn what you can learn from your experiences, and move on.

Make a fresh start.

When is a Good Time for a Fresh Start?

Creating a fresh start is not something you think about only on New Year's Eve when everyone is making their resolutions for the upcoming year.

There are several times during the year that are natural new beginnings; these are just a few:

- New Year's is, of course, the most common time for new beginnings, with resolutions, pledges, setting goals for the year, and so on. It's the beginning of a new year, a perfect time for a fresh start. Get rid of the old, and bring in the new!

- Spring — a time of renewal in nature. It's a time to celebrate that winter is over, that new life is beginning all around us. The grass is turning green again, the flowers are peeking through, and the weather is warming up — this is a great time of year to let go of the old, and to welcome something fresh and new in your life!

- Along with springtime comes the Christian celebration of Easter. Actually, most major religions have a celebration of some sort in the spring. Easter Sunday is celebrated by Christians every year on the first Sunday following the first full moon after the Spring Equinox. Talk about a perfect time for renewal and fresh starts! Regardless of which religion you may practice, this is a great time to reflect on your life and where it is heading, and to incorporate the power of prayer into your reflections.

- The end of the school year and beginning of summer vacation is a good time for introspection, as is the end of summer vacation and beginning of a new school year. Both of these times mark an ending of something old as well as a beginning of something new, and both include a lot of planning, and life events you can look forward to.

- Summer — oh, yes! Almost all kids look forward to summer! It's a perfect time to feel the sun on your face, enjoy the glory of the great outdoors, and experience nature's growing season. Grow a new beginning for yourself!

- Fall — when the trees let go of their leaves and the garden dies back. What a great time for letting go of the things that are no longer working for you.

- Winter — the time of the year when nature sleeps. Now this is the time for some serious introspection. Time to rest, time to think, time to plan. What is there to look forward to? What fresh start can you plan for?

So, when would be a good time for *you* to make a fresh start in *your* life? That's up to you.

Pick a time that means something to you — perhaps your favorite time of year, your birthday, or your favorite holiday or time of celebration?

One of my favorite times to re-evaluate my life and to re-set my goals is my birthday. I give a lot of thought to the goals I set — even those I may not have achieved over the past year — and think about what I need to do to achieve my goals during the next year, or what I need to change to achieve those I didn't achieve.

Fresh starts can be an annual, monthly, weekly, or even daily event. Gosh, every day begins with a sunrise, and ends with a sunset. Endings and beginnings — keep thinking ahead — where do you want to go and what do you want to do?

THINK TIME:

When is your favorite time to think about a fresh start?

NOTES • THOUGHTS • IDEAS:

MENTAL EXERCISE FOR MENTAL FITNESS

Knowing your own mind
is the solution to all our problems.

– Lama Thubren Yeshe, Tibetan Monk

Did you physically work out today — do some exercises, take a long walk, go swimming, play a sport, ride your bike?

Did you mentally work out today — do a crossword puzzle, solve any riddles, play any word games?

Did you know that mental exercise is as important to your mind-body health as physical exercise?

So, what are the benefits of mental exercises? For one thing, exercising your brain will increase your creative or lateral thinking capabilities.

Think about this: what would you do if you were on your way to school or to work and the road was closed because of an accident? There is no one there to direct you around the barricade — no one to tell you how to get to where you are trying to go.

What do you do? Are you going to just sit there until the road opens up again? Or, are you going to turn around and go home? Or, are you going to figure out how to get from where you are to where you need to be?

Need Help With Problem-Solving?

In my classes, I use mental exercises to help develop my students' problem-solving skills..

Optical illusions can be used to illustrate that things are not always as they appear to be. Sometimes you have to look closely to understand — to see what something *really* is — you have to dig a little deeper to see the truth, pay close attention to the details. Illusions are a wonderful tool to illustrate perspective — that sometimes you just need to change the way you look at something to better understand it.

A few examples of typical optical illusions:

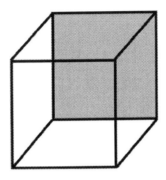

This illusion is based on the concept of a Necker's Cube. Can you tell if the shaded area of this cube is located at the front or the back of the cube? Based on where you focus your attention, the shaded area could be at the front *or* the back.

What is this — do you see a duck or a rabbit?

When you look at this illustration, your brain is going back and forth between recognizing this as a rabbit and a duck.

This is an ambiguous figure, meaning it's both.

This duck-rabbit illusion was created by psychologist Joseph Jastrow in the late 1800s, along with the next illusion, commonly referred to as the Jastrow Illusion.

Can you tell which of the figures is wider — shape A or B?

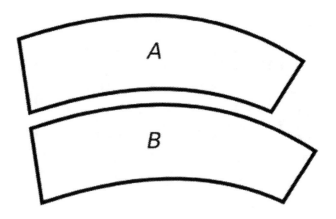

The two figures are identical in size, even though the lower one appears to be larger.

Illusions, in particular, show students that they can be misled, that sometimes they need additional information to solve a problem, that they can be fooled by what they see — and, that they should not jump to conclusions.

Here's an example of why you should try not to jump to conclusions until you get all the information — picture this:

You walk into a room where your best friend is sitting next to your boy/girl-friend, and they seem to be discussing something that's very private. Their heads are close together, and they are both smiling.

You jump to the conclusion that they are plotting against you, or that your best friend is making moves on your boy/girl-friend. Because you are a teenager, you respond emotionally.

You yell at them, and call them names.

Mortified by your behavior, they yell back at you and call *you* names. Your boy/girl-friend storms out of the room and your best friend follows.

The reality: they were planning a surprise birthday party for you because they both love you so much.

By training yourself to think before you react — to look more deeply at situations — you learn to see alternative options.

I also like to use word games, puzzles, brain teasers, and riddles to exercise students' brains, and to encourage them to work together to solve problems.

Someone may come up with an answer that is incorrect, but their answer sparks an idea in someone else's mind who comes with another answer. They work together, and eventually someone will come up with the right answer.

Mental exercises also illustrate that sometimes we learn what doesn't work (remember that chapter on "mistakes" and "happy accidents?").

Exercising your brain by doing any type of mental exercises will condition you to think outside the box, to look at things in an alternative way, and will help you to be able to come up with solutions to problems.

STUDENT CHALLENGE!

So, let's think outside the box!

I have a challenge for you.

Get out a piece of paper and put four dots on it, like corners of a box. It should look like this:

●   ●

●   ●

Now, here's the challenge: Using only three straight lines, connect all four of these dots that kind of look like corners of a box. The tricky part — all three lines must touch another line on each end, they must be straight, and they cannot cross each other.

Take just a few minutes to solve this puzzle.

Need a hint?

I have planted an image of a box in your subconscious mind. By mentioning the word "box" a few times, and telling you the dots are like corners of a box, you now have a mental boundary that has been established. You are trying to fit the three lines inside that boundary, aren't you?

Remember what I said — think outside the box.

Need another hint?

Let's think geometry. Think of a three-sided shape.

A triangle, right? How can you apply that information to help solve the puzzle?

Don't give up too quickly!

Mental exercises help to improve your critical thinking skills. When you are trying to solve problems, it may help to break the problem into smaller pieces and solve each piece. Sometimes the best approach is to eliminate what is not possible. Then, think of other options — what *is* possible?

STUDENT ACTIVITY

Find some brain teasers, riddles, word puzzles, number puzzles, etc. either in books or online. Work alone, or with friends, and see how many of these problems you can solve. Try to do some sort of mental exercise every day!

So! What Did You Do With Those Four Dots?

Is this the solution you came up with (or a variation of this)?

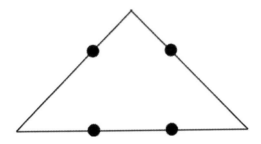

Life will try to place boundaries around you — try to box you in with limitations. Learn to break those boundaries in your life; learn to think outside the box!

THINK TIME:

How has what you have seen distracted you,
misled you, or fooled you in the past?

CHAPTER TWENTY-TWO

A QUICK PEEK AT YOUR SUBCONSCIOUS

I will praise thee; for I am fearfully and wonderfully made:
marvelous are thy works;
and that my soul knoweth right well.
– Psalm139:14

You've already read a lot here about your mind, and the power of your subconscious mind.

I am going to illustrate in this chapter how it works, but first a bit of a review.

The conscious mind and the subconscious are not two separate minds — they are two separate parts of one mind, and they function differently from each other.

The conscious mind is used to reason and make decisions. When you make a choice — regardless of how simple or complex — it is with your conscious mind.

The subconscious works subjectively in the background, without conscious choice and without judgment. The subconscious is amazing; it is always at work — processing information, running the autonomic systems of the body, and leading the conscious mind. Whatever you have programmed into your subconscious will be accepted as real by your subconscious — the subconscious does not distinguish between what is real and what is not.

Let's Take A Test!

I love tests! Don't you? I took an interesting test back in the early 1970s; it consisted of five scenarios that would reveal what was going on in the subconscious mind.

(Note: The following test is based on the one I took way back in the 70s. I have modified the concept so I can use it with teens. It can tell you a lot about yourself — if you take the time to interpret it.)

Get out a piece of paper and a pencil — time for a test!.

Read each of the following scenarios carefully, one at a time, then write down your responses.

Don't over-think these; just write down whatever comes into your mind.

There are no wrong answers to any of these; whatever you write down is the correct response. There should be no test anxiety here! I promise you *will* pass this test!

First, think of your favorite color.

It doesn't matter what the color is, just get a picture of it in your mind. If it's a blend of colors, or a pattern, that's okay. Get a clear image of it — see it in your mind.

Now, write down four words that describe your favorite color that you see in your mind.

Also, if it helps to write a sentence instead of just words, you can do that. Again, there are no incorrect responses.

Now, think of your favorite animal.

It doesn't matter what the animal is, just get a picture of it in your mind. If it's a mythical or imaginary animal, that's okay. Get a clear image of it — see it in your mind.

Now, write down four words that describe your favorite animal that you see in your mind.

Last, if I were to pop in to see you unexpectedly, there is a room in your home that you don't want me to see. It doesn't matter what room it is — and it doesn't have to be *your* room.

Think about that room and why you don't want me to see it, then write down four words that explain why you don't want me to see this room.

So, What Does All Of This Mean?

Let's start with the color.

There is a reason why we all have a favorite color, why we are drawn to that color, why we want to wear that color, wrap ourselves in that color, paint the walls that color, buy a car that color.

When you think of that color, you subconscious goes to work and starts sending messages to your conscious mind.

On a *SUBCONSCIOUS* level, right *NOW*, at this point in time, the words you chose to describe your color are how *YOU* see *YOURSELF*.

Now, the animal.

There is a reason we all have a favorite animal, why we are drawn to that animal, why we have a sort of admiration or connection to that animal.

When you think of that animal, your subconscious goes to work and starts sending messages to your conscious mind.

Again, on a *SUBCONSCIOUS* level, right *NOW*, at this point in time, the words you used to describe the animal are how *YOU THINK* the *WORLD SEES YOU*; the image you *think* you project. Not necessarily how the world *does* see you, just how *you think* the world sees you.

Interestingly, the words are usually not the same on these two lists. In all the years I have been giving this test to students, I've only had a couple of students with all four responses the same, a few more with three that are the same, a few more with two that are the same, and a little more frequently, one is the same.

Clearly, the way we see ourselves (our image of who we are), and the way we think others see us, (the image we think we project to the world), is very different.

Think about that.

Now, about that room you don't want me to see.

There are things about ourselves that we want to keep private, that we don't want anyone to know about us. Those words you wrote down are the things you want to keep to yourself — the things about yourself that you don't want to share.

Can you guess what the #1 response is to this one?

"Messy."

Kids think their lives are messy.

Let's face it — life is messy, and not just for kids!

I have had students who tell me there is no room that they wouldn't let me see, that they wouldn't care if I saw any room.

This is a correct answer for these students. There are those who are very open and have nothing they feel they need to keep to themselves.

While this is a fairly simplistic test, it does give you something to think about — some insight into your subconscious mind and how it works.

The hard part...

You need to figure out what all those words mean *to you.*

THINK TIME:

> *How is your self-image different from*
> *the image you think you project?*

NOTES • THOUGHTS • IDEAS:

CHAPTER TWENTY-THREE

LEARN TO INTERPRET YOUR DREAMS and WHAT SYMBOLS REPRESENT TO YOU

Truth did not come into the world naked,
but it came in type and images.
One will not receive the truth in any other way...
– The Gospel of St. Philip

Carl Jung, noted psychiatrist/psychoanalyst, and a favorite of mine, was of the opinion that the human psyche — the conscious and subconscious mind — held deep within it a "collective unconscious," and that stored within this were instinctive patterns formed by human experiences throughout the ages.

Jung believed that there were images, or symbols, that were recognized and represented universally.

There are certain symbols that we all recognize and associate with certain things. For example, this heart shape ♥ is universally recognized to represent the heart, or love, even though it is only abstractly shaped like a real heart.

Symbols, icons, logos, ideograms, and graphic gestalts play an important role in communication and marketing as much today as they did in the past when people communicated through drawings instead of written words.

Did you know that logos were originally developed to represent a type of business in a time when few people could read? If a person were looking for a barber, they knew to look for the iconic red and white striped pole. One of the first things a business, organization or group does is develop a logo to create a quickly and easily recognized identity.

Who today does not recognize their favorite restaurant's logo, or that of their favorite sports team, or clothing brand? Can you picture the logo of your favorite breakfast cereal, or the symbol that your favorite music group uses on all of their tee shirts?

Interpretation

Symbols have become an integral part of everyday language, and part of our everyday lives.

So, how do you know what the symbols in your dreams and visions mean to you?

Take another look at those words you wrote down in the exercise in chapter 22. Think about them.

Do they mean anything specific to you? Do you understand what they symbolize to you? Try to determine what those individual words specifically represent to *you* — it's kind of like interpreting a dream.

While you could refer to an outside source to get a basic idea of what the words or symbols might represent abstractly — as suggested by Jung — you shouldn't have someone else interpret your words for you. You have to do it yourself.

Based on your life experience, the words you wrote down will symbolize something different to you than to someone else. For example, the word "tree" might represent "family" to me, but "strength" to you.

Another example: if your favorite color is yellow, and one of the words you wrote on your list to describe that color is "bright," you now have to determine what that word specifically means to *you*. Does it symbolize your bright personality — that when you walk into a room, you light it up? Or does it mean you are bright — meaning intelligent?

Figure out what your subconscious is telling you about yourself. If you know you are pretty smart, the interpretation may be "intelligent."

If you know that people like you, and that when you walk into a room, people turn and smile at you, the interpretation may be that you "light up a room."

Again, it's important that you analyze the symbols yourself. One of the problems with relying on someone else to interpret the meaning, or just reading a book to see what it tells you the symbol represents, is that the meanings of symbols or icons can vary from age group to age group, culture to culture, religion to religion.

So, go back to your list. Take one word at a time and analyze it. Think about it — and write down what that word specifically means to *you*.

There are *so* many reference books for interpreting symbols and dreams — some good, some not. If you need help getting started, I have included the titles of some books I like at the back of this book. Just remember, these offer abstract references, you still need to figure out for yourself what they mean to *you*.

THINK TIME:

Write out your dreams for a few days —
include as many details as you can remember.
Take some time to figure out what the images mean to you.

NOTES • THOUGHTS • IDEAS:

PART THREE

THE PRACTICE OF MEDITATION

Let the words of my mouth,
and the meditation of my heart,
be acceptable in thy sight, O Lord,
my strength, and my redeemer.
— Psalm 19:14

mrs. neal's not-so-conventional meditation class for teens...

Wisdom begins in wonder.

– Socrates, philosopher / teacher

I created and developed this not-so-conventional meditation class many years ago because students were eager to learn how to use the relaxation techniques I had discussed in a graphic arts class.

Students were curious and I love to teach — it seemed like a good idea!

One of the most important things I learned from my own child is that kids ask a lot of questions — and they always seem to want to know "why."

When he was just a little boy, my son asked me that age-old question, "Why is the sky blue?" We used to spend a lot of time outdoors, looking at the sky, watching clouds, talking about the changes in the sky from different types of weather, or at different times of the day.

It came as no surprise when the question came up, "Why is the sky blue?" I explained to him that it had to do with how light from the sun is diffused through the atmosphere, and how the atmosphere affects the different bands of light waves. He didn't need a lengthy, detailed, highly-scientific answer, he just needed a simple explanation; he was satisfied with that answer.

After I taught my first meditation class, students wanted to know why: why *how* you breathe is such a big deal, why their fingers tingled, why they felt like they were dreaming, why one student fell asleep.

They wanted — no, they *needed* — to know the science behind it. I pulled out all of my old books, and bought a few new ones — and then I started to put some classes together that would answer their questions.

As I taught more classes, I would talk to students to see if there were other questions they had.

Over the years, my meditation program has developed into the program I teach today — complete with my best answers to all of their questions.

If I didn't know the answer, I told them so.

I also told them I would find an answer for them, or — more often than not — I would challenge them to find an answer.

I base my classes on the science behind each topic I teach, and on my personal spirituality.

No compromises. I have found that my students appreciate the honesty and knowledge I bring to share with them. And, they appreciate learning the *hows* and *whys*.

The How, When, Where, Why, And More Of Meditation

Several students requested that I include the *how, when, where* and *why* to use meditation. I do get a lot of questions about this, so, here are my answers to some of those most-asked questions from students.

How...

As I have mentioned elsewhere, there are many ways of practicing meditation; the class I teach is a very basic and easy-to-learn method — especially for teens.

I have found that if I keep it simple, students are more willing to try it.

After you get the basics down, you may choose to try different, or more advanced forms of meditation.

One of my students pointed out — and asked that I include in this book — that it's important to be aware that when you are in an active state — when your brain waves are at higher levels of activity — it may take longer and be harder to achieve a meditative state than when you are already in a relaxed state.

Chapter 27 includes a guided meditation, which will go into more details about *how* to meditate.

When...

Teenagers are emotional — it's your brain (remember reading about that?). Because of this, you need to de-stress yourself once in a while.

When you are feeling stressed or upset — for whatever reason — just taking a breath will help in the moment. However, if the opportunity exists, meditation is a great option for relaxing, and calming yourself down.

Another time that meditation is good to use is before taking a test. Studies have shown that if students can put themselves into the same state that they were in when they were studying, they will recall more information, and do better on the test.

(It's also great for when you are preparing to study!)

If you have a hard time getting to sleep, try using meditation. The relaxation exercises used in meditation will help to slow down your brain waves, which is what happens naturally when you go to sleep.

Teens, in general, do not get enough sleep. Take another look at the section on sleep in chapter two, and how much sleep you should be getting. Do you get enough? Why not?

Using meditation not only can help with sleep, it also can serve as a sort of "power nap" when you just need to "recharge." For example, if you have an after-school job, or play sports after school, or have other responsibilities, taking a few minutes to get into a meditative state will give you the energy to get through the rest of your day!

Where...

The environment you choose will affect your meditation. This topic has been touched on in other chapters that discussed the body and brain resonating with the frequencies around you.

Find a quiet place, if possible, with few distractions.

Be aware of your surroundings. The people, colors, and objects around you will have an impact on the quality of your meditation. Try to find a space with calming colors — pastels, blues, greens — and a space with minimal objects.

Solitude is nice — preferably with no people or other distractions. Turn off the phone, TV, blaring radio, etc.

Soft music is nice; loud, pounding music is not.

The ideal place is a place you can use whenever you want — like a corner in your room that you can convert to a meditation space. All you need is a comfortable, cozy place to sit. A CD player is nice for that soft, soothing music, if you'd like. Scent is an option, too, but not necessary. Light an incense stick or use a drop of essential oil on a cotton ball (more on that later).

A busy, noisy environment will not be conducive to a peaceful meditation. If you can't do anything about the external noise, wear headphones, and turn the volume down!

Why...

Gosh, where to begin!

There are *so* many benefits to using meditation — many of which have been discussed in other chapters in this book.

One of the best is that meditation will trigger the release of those feel-good endorphins! It just makes you *feel* good!

My students have told me they have used meditation to help them to sleep, to control their anger, to focus their thoughts and to study, to deal with their stress, and to pray.

In addition to reducing stress, other benefits include gaining a clearer mental focus, a stronger immune system, and improving your self-control.

A point I stress in class is that when you are using meditation, *you* are staying in control of *your* mind and *your* body the entire time. No *one*, no *thing* takes that control away from you.

And More...

I do use aromatherapy in class when I can.

I explain that scent is a powerful tool — and that our sense of smell, a more primitive sense, not only evokes memories, but also can induce relaxation.

There's a bit of science here, too. When we breathe in a pleasant scent, the olfactory bulb (scent gland) — part of the limbic system — which is located just behind the bridge of our nose sends a message to the receptors in the brain that trigger the release of those feel-good chemicals.

I place a drop of an essential oil on a cotton ball to hand out in class. The oils are a good quality (from Spiritual Sky Incense in New Zealand — I use their oils to ensure students don't have a reaction to the oils). The scents are selected for their relaxation qualities — lavender, musk, sandalwood, etc.

As I am beginning the class, I hand a scented cotton ball to each student. As I place the scented cotton ball into their hands, I have an opportunity to connect with each student.

As a side note here, I think God uses this opportunity to guide me to students who need attention.

I also like to use music in class.

I bring a selection of CDs with me that would be appropriate for meditation — soft, gentle music, flutes, acoustic guitars, nature sounds, classical with the sounds of the ocean, and so on.

I then ask for a student to be my volunteer, and have that student select which CD we will listen to during the class.

This gives me an opportunity to point out that volunteering can be a good thing!

Next, we talk about the type of music we use in class, and why. The type of music is soft and soothing, with no words.

As discussed in previous chapters, the body and brain resonate with the frequencies around them — that includes music.

I must share these two brief stories about the music.

First story:

I love the Rolling Stones' music (yes, I am that old), and I love classical music. I have a CD of a philharmonic orchestra playing the Stones' music. However, I can't use it for meditation because I know the words to the songs, and I find myself singing along in my head. It's a great CD, but it's not effective for meditation.

Second story:

I was playing a classical-type CD in class one evening, and I had gotten to the part of the class where I go through a guided meditation. As I was guiding the students through the relaxation exercise — and the CD had come to a particular track of music — I noticed that some of the students were flinching a little, opening their eyes and looking around, and acting a little startled. I asked if there was a problem. I was told that, that particular piece of music was a sound track from a horror movie.

I never used that CD again.

An Interesting Thing Happens...

In the places where I teach classes on a regular basis, I have found that students begin to take ownership of the class.

There are some things we talk about at the beginning of each class — why we use music in class, why we use the type of music we use, what effect the scented cotton balls have — those students who have been in several of my classes not only will volunteer to answer the questions, they are the ones who also get involved and participate the most in class.

These are the students I expect to teach the class someday!

STUDENT CHALLENGE:

Students ask me all the time to give them a list of books or websites that they can study to learn more.

I have included a list of a few of my favorite books — *recommended reading* — at the back of this book.

If you are interested in learning more about meditation, spirituality, metaphysics, philosophy, or a few of the topics covered in my classes, check out a book or two and read them.

As for the websites, I challenge you to search for the information you are specifically interested in researching. Just use caution when you visit some of the sites. As you probably already know, there is a lot of garbage out there!

THINK TIME:

How, when, where and why do you use meditation?

NOTES • THOUGHTS • IDEAS:

CHAPTER TWENTY-FIVE

LIFE FORCE, CHI, QI, PRANA, ENERGY FIELD, WHATEVER...

What lies behind us and what lies before us
are tiny matters compared to what lies within us.
– Ralph Waldo Emerson, author

The essence of who you are does not end with the outer layer of your skin. You have a life force within you, which also may be referred to as your life force, chi, qi, prana, or energy field. This life force is something you can feel within and around you.

Let me give you an example:
Rub your hands together.
What are you creating?
(Friction.)
What does friction produce?
(Heat.)
What does heat do to matter?
(Expands it and makes it move faster.)

As you are creating this heat, you also are focusing your attention on your hands. Now pull them apart just a little bit, holding them close to each other. You may have a sensation of holding a soft ball or balloon between your hands.

Now, close your eyes and bring your right hand up by your throat, but don't touch your throat. Can you feel the heat, pressure, or tingling in your hand?

Now move your hand up your face — without actually touching your face — and feel the warmth and pressure from your hand.

Pause over your forehead, then move your hand to the top of your head. You should be able to sense where your hand is as it moves from your throat to top of your head.

What you feel is your life force — or whatever you choose to call it. Don't worry if you can't sense it right away — it may take a while to get used to feeling it. The more you practice, the easier it will become.

Another example of how this energy is sensed:

Have you ever been standing in line — like at a store — and you just *know* someone is standing behind you? You don't have to turn around to look, you just *know*.

Or, have you ever been standing next to someone, and you get an uneasy feeling, and you need to move away from them?

Because an interruption in the flow of your energy can cause stress, it also can interfere with your meditation.

When you practice meditation, or go through a relaxation exercise, you may be able to feel your life force move through your body.

The relaxation exercise I teach in my class is designed to help raise your awareness of this life force, especially when you relax one part of your body at a time, then move on to the next.

The more you practice, the more aware you will become of *your* life force.

STUDENT CHALLENGE!

When I have a discussion about our life forces in my classes, it usually leads to the topics of acupuncture, acupressure, energy vortices, and chakras. If this is something you are truly interested in learning more about, I suggest you look it up!

THINK TIME:

Are you aware of your life force?

NOTES • THOUGHTS • IDEAS:

CHAPTER TWENTY-SIX

CREATING YOUR PLACE OF PEACE

And now here is my secret, a very simple secret:
it is only with the heart that one can see rightly;
what is essential is invisible to the eye.

– Antoine de Saint-Exupéry, author

Close your eyes — well, read this first, then close your eyes.

Think about the ideal place you would create — where you would choose to go if you wanted to find a little peace and quiet; a place you would go for solitude or relaxation.

This place can be anyplace you choose. It's a place that you create and you control, where no *thing* and no *one* could get to you. This place belongs to *you*, and in this place, you are *safe*.

You should try to make this place as real as possible by putting as much detail into its creation as possible.

When you visualize this place, imagine that you are looking all the way around you — look up, look down, look all around you — try to see every detail that matters to you.

The more details you can include when you are creating this place, the more real it will seem to you when you begin to visualize it.

Remember that the subconscious mind does not recognize the difference between what is real and what is not. When you visualize this place, your subconscious will accept it as *real*.

The method of meditation I teach includes creating a place of peace. I believe it is important for my students to feel safe and secure in their "Place of Peace," so we create it on a very personal level, and I always stress that in this place, you are safe.

Get out a piece of paper. Make a list something like this:

Where is your place of peace?
What is the weather like?
What season is it?
What is the time of day?
What do you hear in this place?
What do you smell?
What do you taste?
What do you see?
What can you touch, or what touches you?
How does this place make you feel?
What will you name this place?

Now, following the outline below, create your place of peace using that list you just made.

Let's Create Your Place of Peace!

- Begin by choosing a location.
  Where is your ideal place of peace? Would you choose a forest, a beach, your backyard, your bedroom? Be specific, and remember that because your subconscious doesn't care if it's a real place or not, it can be anywhere you choose.

- What is the weather like?
  Even if you choose to be on a beach, if you like snow blowing wildly, you can have it. Decide the ideal weather you want in your special place.

- Which season is your favorite?
  Again, if you love the colors and smells of fall, but want a hot, sunny day, that's okay.

- What is the time of day would you choose?
  Are you a morning person, or do you prefer the dark
  twilight hours? It's *your* happy place, it's *your* choice.

- What would you hear in this place?
  Think about the sounds you might hear in your special
  place — the ocean, the rustle of leaves in the trees, birds
  singing, or soft music. You choose what you want to hear.

- What would you smell?
  Does you happy place smell like pine trees, mountain air,
  the ocean, freshly-baked cookies?

- What might you taste?
  Do you have some of those freshly-baked cookies with you?
  Or perhaps you taste the salt of the ocean?

- What would you see in this place that you have created?
  What will you place here? Do you have a vase of fresh
  flowers on a table, or do you see snow-capped mountains?
  Is there a picture of someone you love on the wall, or do
  you see seagulls against a bright blue sky?

- What might you touch, or what touches you?
  What can you feel? Can you feel the roughness of the bark
  of a tree against your back, or a plush carpet under your
  feet, or the softness of the grass where you are sitting? Are
  there flowers brushing against your legs as you walk a quiet
  path? Can you feel the soft fur and vibration of the purring
  of your favorite little kitten sitting on your lap?

- How does this place make you feel?
  When you visualize yourself in this special place of peace
  that you have created, how do you *feel*?

  Finally, set a trigger for this place.
  A trigger is something that sets something else in motion.
  Set the trigger for your place of peace by creating a name for this
  place. Choose a name that means something to you.

  Depending on your mood or other factors, your happy place
  might change from time to time.
  That's okay, just re-create it based on how you are feeling!

  Now, the next time you are in need of a little peace and quiet,
  close your eyes and think of the name of your happy place, or say it
  out loud, then take a deep breath and imagine yourself *there*.

STUDENT CHALLENGE:

Whether you think you are artistic or not, try creating your place of peace — or "happy" place — as a tangible model!

This is an exercise I like to do with students to reinforce the reality of this place to the subconscious mind.

What I do is dump a bunch of crayons, markers, colored pencils, white and colored papers of various sizes and weights, cotton balls, scissors, modeling clay and dough, pieces of chipboard or cardboard, glue and glue sticks, tape, glitter, paints, and other assorted art supplies onto a table.

I lead the class in a relaxation exercise, then have them go through the process of creating their place of peace on a piece of paper, using the same outline as above.

When they reach their relaxed state, I turn them loose with the art supplies and have them create a model of some sort of their place of peace using whichever methods they choose.

Here's *your* challenge: gather some art supplies and create a model of *your* happy place!

THINK TIME:

Create and visualize your Place of Peace...

mrs. neal's BASIC GUIDED MEDITATION EXERCISE

Give ear to my words, O Lord, consider my meditation.
– Psalm 5:1

About The Guided Meditation

Let's review. Here are a few things you might want to keep in mind before beginning a meditation. Some of this information has been discussed in detail elsewhere in this book; if you are unclear about what any of this means, go back and re-read it.

- Above all, always remember that you have the gift of free will. *You* get to choose how much you participate in this exercise.

- Your body and brain will resonate with the frequencies of your environment. If you are in a noisy room with loud music, you will find it difficult to relax. Find a quiet place to sit or lie down before you begin this meditation.

- If you would like, burn incense, or use essential oils to scent the air with a relaxing scent. Your sense of smell is powerful. By inhaling scents such as lavender, sandalwood, or musk, your brain will release serotonin to help you relax.

- Music is incredibly powerful. Lyrics to songs are fed into your subconscious mind, so be aware of the music you choose. When meditating or reducing stress, listen to music with no words. Again, remember that your mind and body will resonate with those frequencies around you.

- If you would like, you can block the frequencies around you, or close your circuits. By that I mean — bring your fingertips together, cross your ankles and touch the tip of your tongue to the roof of your mouth, just behind your front teeth, on that "ridge-y" part. *(This is one of the pressure points that helps with relaxation.)*

- Sit up straight. There is a trick we learned in etiquette class way back when I was in school — pretend there is a string tapped into the top of your head and pull up on it. This helps to align your body, and opens your chest. Also, relax your tummy muscles so you can breathe deeply.

- Keep in mind that as your brain waves slow down, there will be a release of a chemical in your body that may make you feel tingly, floaty, or detached from your body. This is called sleep paralysis, or pseudo paralysis, and it happens naturally when you go to sleep.

- If you have been in one of my classes, you know that we begin with a lesson before doing the meditation exercise. You can go back and read one, or just think of what you want to get out of the meditation before you begin. If you are doing this with friends, have a discussion about one of the lessons!

- A side effect of meditation is that you may fall asleep. While you are learning, practice this someplace where that won't be a problem!

OK! Let's get to the part that all my students like the most:

The Guided Meditation

First, sit up straight! Take a few nice deep breaths, breathing in through your nose. Relax your belly muscles so your lungs can fill completely. Don't just pant or breathe shallowly with the top of your lungs. Breathe deeply into your lungs. By inhaling through your nose, air rushes past those nerve endings in your nasal passages and stimulates them sending a message to your brain to release a chemical that helps to relax your body.

You should feel yourself begin to relax a bit.

NOTE: You can do this simple movement — close your circuits and breathe deeply — anytime and anyplace that you need to induce the relaxation response.

Now, you will begin to intentionally slow your brain waves down. This is nothing your body doesn't already know how to do. Remember that your brain waves are fluctuating throughout the day, and they slow way down every night when you go to sleep — in meditation, you're just doing it with awareness.

Start this process by getting your breathing into a rhythm. Counting can help with this — count to four as you inhale deeply, then pause a moment, and count to eight as you slowly exhale.

It is important to find your own rhythm — to find what feels natural for you. If that means counting to three as you inhale, and to six as you exhale — do that.

Stay focused on your breath. Be aware of how it feels when you fill your lungs with air, then how it feels as your body releases the air and it leaves your body.

Continue to count in your head as you get into a rhythm with your breath.

As your breathing falls into a rhythm, your heart rate will begin to slow down, and your brain waves will begin to slow down — natural body processes.

Now, to slow your brain waves down a little more and deepen this state, try to visualize a place where you would choose to go to find some peace and quiet, calmness, serenity, solitude — a place where you can relax.

Use your trigger to recall your place of peace that you created in chapter 26.

Remember that your subconscious does not distinguish between what is real and what is not, so you can have whatever you want in this place, and it will be real to your subconscious.

This is a place that you create and you control — this is a place where no *one* and no *thing* can get to you. This place belongs to *you* — and in this place, you are *safe*.

Breathing deeply and exhaling slowly, stay focused on your breath and visualize this place where you find peace, where you are safe.

Breathing becomes rhythmic, your heart rate slows down, brain waves slow down...

When distracting thoughts come into your mind, or you hear distracting sounds, come back to your breathing. Stay focused on your breath and that place where you find peace — where you feel safe.

Now, to slow your brain waves down a little more and deepen this state even further, you will begin to relax your body. Rather than trying to do the whole thing at once, we'll break it down and do a little bit at a time.

Begin by bringing your attention to just the muscles in your feet. Focus on just that part of your body, then consciously relax just those muscles. With your next deep breath, let the tension or tightness drain from your feet, and imagine that the tension or tightness is going through the floor and into the earth — imagine it is draining away from you.

Now bring your attention to just those muscles in your lower legs. Focus on just that part of your body, then consciously relax those muscles. With your next deep breath, as you exhale slowly, let any tightness or stress drain from your legs and move through your feet, and imagine it is going through the floor, and into the earth.

Staying focused on your breath, visualize that place where you find peace — where you feel safe.

Now bring your attention to just the muscles in your upper legs. Focus on just that part of your body, then consciously relax those muscles. With your next deep breath, as you exhale slowly, let any stress or tension drain from your upper legs, and flow through your lower legs, move through your feet, and go through the floor, and into the earth.

Next bring your attention to just those muscles in your lower torso — your tummy muscles and lower back. Focus on just that part of your body, then consciously relax those muscles. With your next deep breath, as you exhale slowly, let any tension or tightness drain from your lower torso, and flow through your legs, move through your feet, and go through the floor, into the earth.

Now, bring your attention to just the muscles in your upper torso — your chest, your upper back, and especially those muscles across your shoulders where we tend to carry so much tension. Focus on just that part of your body, then consciously relax those muscles. With your next deep breath, as you exhale slowly, let any tightness and stress drain from your torso, flow through your legs, move through your feet, and go through the floor, into the earth.

Staying focused on your breath, visualize that place where you find peace — where you feel safe.

Next bring your attention all the muscles in your arms and hands. Focus on just that part of your body, then consciously relax those muscles. With your next deep breath, as you exhale slowly, let any stress and tension drain from your arms and drip off your fingertips, drain from your torso and flow through your legs, move through your feet, and go through the floor, into the earth.

And now, bring your attention to your head — all the muscles in your head. Focus on just that part of your body, then consciously relax your scalp, forehead, eyes, ears, cheeks, tongue, jaw, neck...

With your next deep breath, as you exhale slowly, let any remaining tightness, tension, *stress* drain from your head, flow down your arms, drip off your fingertips, drain from your torso and flow through your legs, move through your feet, and go through the floor, into the earth and drain away.

When you have completely relaxed your body, stay focused on your breath.

Recall the trigger you have set for your place of peace. Visualize that place where you find peace, where you feel safe.

Step into this place.

When you come to this place, you plant the seeds into your subconscious that you want to harvest into your life.

Consider any goals you want to achieve, habits you want to change, problems you want to solve, obstacles you want to overcome, prayers you want to send — you choose.

You come to this place, sit and be still.

You choose how long you stay in this state of relaxed meditation, and how you use it. It always should be your choice.

And, you should feel free to modify any part of this to whatever feels comfortable to you.

If you prefer not to use music, don't use it. If you prefer not to use scent, don't. If you prefer to do this exercise outside, by all means, do that! *(Personally, I love being outdoors to meditate.)*

You may have noticed that my relaxation exercise has a sort of rhythm to it — there's a reason for that. This is one way of moving your life force (chapter 25) and remaining grounded, so to speak.

It also brings your awareness to your body.

In class — because of time restraints — I am silent for one minute after I say, "Sit and be still." That one minute seems like a much longer time to most students.

When you bring yourself to your place of peace — to that place of stillness within you where you find inner silence — you will discover how much your mind can process in a very short amount of time.

Your mind is so amazing!

A Few Benefits...

Meditating can help to relax you, calm you down, help stimulate or train your mind, sharpen your focus, help you study, release creativity, and *so* much more — all while remaining aware of your surroundings, and staying in control of your mind and your body.

As mentioned earlier, one of the side effects of meditation is that you might become so relaxed, you fall asleep.

Considering that most teens don't get enough sleep, I don't see this as a bad thing!

Many of my students have commented over the years on how spending just five to ten minutes a day in a quiet meditation can change a person's whole day — or even their life.

(me, smiling.)

Because I have received so many nice comments from
my students over the years, I have included some of them
in this book. I am always so humbled
by what my students share with me!

THINK TIME:

Meditate. Sit and be still...

NOTES • THOUGHTS • IDEAS:

NOTES • THOUGHTS • IDEAS:

PART FOUR

CLOSING THOUGHTS

I have chosen to be happy because it is good for my health.

– Voltaire, author

NOTES • THOUGHTS • IDEAS:

CHAPTER TWENTY-EIGHT

A FEW OF MY FAVORITE "THINKING" QUOTES...

Blessed is the man that walketh not in the counsel of the ungodly,
nor standeth in the way of sinners, nor sitteth in the seat of the
scornful. But his delight is in the law of the Lord;
and in his law doth he meditate day and night.

– Psalm 1:1-2

Perhaps you have noticed that I like positive, thought-provoking, encouraging quotations. I use them frequently in class.

I had a wall in my pantry in an old house where I used to live where I would tape little scraps of paper with quotes I liked. Whenever I would find myself feeling a little discouraged, or upset, or stressed, or angry, or whatever — I would go and stand in my pantry and read my wall. I called it my "Inspiration Wall."

After spending just a few minutes standing there reading my wall, I always came out of my pantry feeling more positive about my life, and whatever it was that was bothering me went away.

I decided to share some of my favorite quotes from my "Inspiration Wall" with you. Pick *your* favorites!

Fear thou not; for I am with thee:
be not dismayed; for I am thy God:
I will strengthen thee; yea, I will help thee;
yea, I will uphold thee with
the right hand of my righteousness.

– Isaiah 41:10

Believe you can and you're halfway there.

– Theodore Roosevelt

*Everybody is a genius. But if you judge a fish by its
ability to climb a tree, it will live its whole life believing it is stupid.*

– Unknown ((falsely attributed to Einstein)

We know what we are, but know not what we may be.

– William Shakespeare

*This is my commandment,
That ye love one another, as I have loved you.*

– Jesus, in John 15:12

To the mind that is still, the whole universe surrenders.

– Lao Tzu

*Happiness resides not in possessions, and not in gold,
happiness dwells in the soul.*

– Democritus

*Nurture your mind with great thoughts, for you
will never go any higher than you think."*

– Benjamin Disraeli

*Success does not consist in never making blunders, but
in never making the same one the second time.*

– H.W. Shaw

*Whatever you can do, or dream you can do, begin it.
Boldness has genius, power and magic in it.*

– Johann Wolfgang von Goethe

*Stand in awe, and sin not:
commune with your own heart upon your bed, and be still.*

– Psalm 4:4

Thinking: the talking of the soul with itself.
– Plato

My mouth shall speak of wisdom;
and the meditation of my heart shall be of understanding.
– Psalm 49:3

With self-discipline most anything is possible.
– Theodore Roosevelt

Out of difficulties grow miracles.
– Jean de la Bruyere

This above all, to thine own self be true,
And it follows as the night the day,
Thou canst not then be false to any man.
– from *Hamlet*, by William Shakespeare

Give light, and the darkness will disappear of itself.
– Desiderius Erasmus

Ah, but a man's reach should exceed his grasp,
or what's a heaven for?
– Robert Browning

Science without religion is lame.
Religion without science is blind.
– Albert Einstein [4]

All that is necessary for the triumph of evil
is that good men do nothing.
– Edmund Burke

Anyone can count the seeds in an apple,
but only God can count the number of apples in a seed.
– Robert H. Schuller

People only see what they are prepared to see.
– Ralph Waldo Emerson

Misfortunes often sharpen the genius.
– Ovid

The mind's direction is more important than its progress.
– Joseph Joubert

In order to learn the most important lessons of life,
one must each day surmount a fear.
– Ralph Waldo Emerson

No one stands so straight as he who stoops to help a child.
– Abraham Lincoln

Be still and know that I am God.
– Psalm 46:10

Students have asked me what they are supposed to be thinking about during meditation. Even though I tell them that it is their choice, they sometimes need just a little nudge.

The quotations used in this book are just a few of *my* favorites that I have collected over the years (and was able to use in this book) to help spark students' thought processes, and to give that little inspirational nudge.

THINK TIME:

Create your own "Inspiration Wall."

Use some of these quotations, or find some you like.

Then, stand in front of your wall when you need a little nudge.

NOTES • THOUGHTS • IDEAS:

CHAPTER TWENTY-NINE

A COMMON THREAD — THE GOLDEN RULE...

A new commandment I give unto you, That ye love one another;
as I have loved you, that ye also love one another.

– Jesus, in John 13:34

Okay — One Last Mommy Lecture...

There may be people who will come into your life and try to lead you to believe that their way of thinking, is the *only* way; that their way of life is the *right* way to live.

I pray that you will use the brain God gave you to think about what they are trying to sell you before you buy it.

As I have mentioned elsewhere in this book, I am a Christian. I was brought up as a Christian, I read the Bible, I believe what I read, and I pray every day.

As a Christian, I was brought up with the old concept of *The Golden Rule* — "Do unto others as you would have others do unto you" — the guideline by which we all should be living our lives.

I do my best to live by *The Golden Rule* — a concept that has been around for thousands of years. Way back around 600-800 B.C.E., Homer wrote in his epic book, *The Odyssey*: "I will be as careful for you as I should be for myself in the same need."

An ancient Egyptian writing states, "Do for one who may do for you, that you may cause him thus to do." This is from *The Tale of the Eloquent Peasant* (translated by R.B. Parkinson), and it dates back to around 1800 B.C.E.; it is considered to be perhaps the earliest version of *The Golden Rule* ever written.

When I was young — and in the midst of studying theology (monotheism *and* polytheism) — I noticed that there seemed to be a common thread in *all* religions. It didn't matter what the religion was, there was a law that paralleled *The Golden Rule.* (You also may hear this referred to as the *Ethic of Reciprocity.*)

I want to share with you that *common thread* I found through my studies on this topic — how each religion states their law, or their version of *The Golden Rule:*

Christianity

- *Therefore all things whatsoever ye would that men should do to you, do ye even so to them: for this is the law and the prophets.*

  – Jesus, in Matthew 7:12

- *And as ye would that men should do to you, do ye also to them likewise.*

  – Jesus, in Luke 6:31

Judaism

- *Thou shalt love thy neighbor as thyself.*

  – Leviticus 19:18

- *What is hateful to you, do not to your fellow man. That is the entire Law; all the rest is commentary.*

  – Talmud, Chabbat 31a

- *And what you hate, do not do to any one.*

  – Tobit 4:15 4

Hinduism/Brahmanism

- *This is the sum of duty: Do naught unto others which would cause you pain if done to you.*

  – Mahabharata 5: 1517

Buddhism

- *Hurt not others in ways that you yourself would find hurtful.*

  – Udana-Varga 5.18

- *...a state that is not pleasing or delightful to me, how could I inflict that upon another?*

  – Samyutta NIkaya

Taoism

- *Regard your neighbor's gain as your own gain and your neighbor's loss as your own loss.*

  – Lao Tau, T'ai Shang Kan Yin P'ien

- *To those who are good to me, I am good; to those who are not good to me, I am also good. Thus all get to be good.*

  – Lao Tau, T'ai Shang Kan Yin P'ien

Sikhism

- *I am a stranger to no one; and no one is a stranger to me. I am a friend to all.*

  – Guru Granth Sahib

- *Do not create enmity with anyone as God is within everyone.*

  – Guru Granth Sahib

Native Spirituality

- *Respect for all life is the foundation.*

  – Chief Dan George

- *We are as much alive as we keep the earth alive.*

  – Chief Dan George

Confucianism

- *Surely it is the maxim of loving-kindness:*
  Do not unto others what you would not have them do unto you.
  – Analects 15:23

- *Tse-kung asked, 'Is there one word that can serve as a principle*
  of conduct for life?' Confucius replied, 'It is the word 'shu' —
  reciprocity. Do not impose on others what you yourself do not desire.'
  – Doctrine of the Mean 13.3

- *Try your best to treat others as you would wish to be treated*
  yourself, and you will find that this is the shortest way to
  benevolence.
  – Mencius VII.A.4

Islam

- *No one of you is a believer until he desires for his brother that*
  which he desires for himself.
  – Sunnah

Zoroastrianism

- *That nature alone is good which refrains from doing unto another*
  whatsoever is not good for itself.
  – Dadistan-i-dinik 94:5

- *Whatever is disagreeable to yourself do not do unto others."*
  – Shayast-na-Shayast 13:29 5

Baha'i Faith

- *Lay not on any soul a load that you would not wish to be laid upon you, and desire not for anyone the things you would not desire for yourself.*

  – Baha'u'llah

- *Blessed is he who preferreth his brother before himself.*

  – Baha'u'llah

- *And if thine eyes be turned towards justice, choose thou for thy neighbour that which thou choosest for thyself.*

  – Epistle to the Son of the Wolf

Unitarianism

- *We affirm and promote respect for the interdependent web of all existence of which we are a part.*

  – Unitarian principle

Jainism

- *In happiness and suffering, in joy and grief, we should regard all creatures as we regard our own self.*

  – Lord Mahavira, 24th Tirthankara

- *Therefore, neither does he [a sage] cause violence to others nor does he make others do so.*

  – Acarangasutra 5.101-2

- *A man should wander about treating all creatures as he himself would be treated.*

  – Sutrakritanga 1.11.33

We — as human beings — are expected to treat each other the way we expect others to treat us; respect begets respect.

Remember some of the other lessons in this book — that as a teenager, your brain is not fully developed; that you can be misled or fooled into thinking something is real or true when it isn't; that you have to choose your own path in life; that sometimes you have to take a step back, take a breath, and try to see the big picture; that *you* are responsible for *your* decisions.

Your teenage years and into your early 20s — is a time of discovery. You are figuring out who you are, and where you want to go with your life. It's normal for you to want to try new things, explore new ideas.

I caution you: be careful. Take time to think before you act.

This is also an age when you can easily be misled.

Sadly, there are people who will try to take advantage of that — people who will not have your best interests in mind. They only will be interested in furthering their own agenda.

If someone is trying to lead you down a path you know in your heart — in your gut — is the wrong path for *you*, walk away from them.

And, regardless of your personal beliefs regarding faith or spirituality, if what that person is trying to get you to do does not parallel *The Golden Rule,* RUN away from them!

THINK TIME:

> *Think about what The Golden Rule means to you.*

SHARING KNOWLEDGE...

> *The greatest good you can do for another*
> *is not just to share your riches*
> *but to reveal to him his own.*
> – Benjamin Disraeli, British Statesman

We begin learning about the world around us from the time we are conceived, and we continue to learn from everyone and everything we are exposed to or influenced by for the rest of our lives.

I have always believed that we are all teachers, and we are all students — throughout our lives. I also believe that any time we cross someone's path, we either will learn something from them, or we will teach them something.

This learning can come from our parents, our siblings and other family members, friends and neighbors, our school teachers and classmates, the people we meet in stores, libraries, and church, as well as from books, television, movies, games, internet, and so on.

We are surrounded by so much knowledge — we can't help but absorb some of it when it is all around us.

(This also ties in well with Jung's concept of a collective unconscious, don't you think?)

Students Do Share What They Have Learned In Class!

I expect my students to share the knowledge they gain from being in my classes, and I expect them to share my CD (and now my book) with their friends and family.

Over the years, I have had quite a few students who have studied with me and who have been in enough of my classes that they can *teach* my class. And, I know that some of them do! I love to hear that they are sharing their knowledge!

I know that some of them already have shared their knowledge because they let me know when I see them that they have used what they learned in my class to teach someone else how to meditate.

One example who comes to mind is student who happened to be a bull rider. He had been in a couple of my classes and had a copy of my CD he was using to practice on his own. I had worked with him on visualization to help him improve his bull-riding skills.

I ran into him several months after the last class we had together, and he shared with me that he and his buddies would go out to his truck before their bull riding events and they would meditate — they all had improved their skills.

Picture that!

Another one of my students asked me to be sure to mention that this program works with families, too. He had been in several of my classes while in a court-ordered program, and had taken a CD home with him. He had listened to it regularly and shared it with his family.

He told me how my class had helped him to build a better relationship with his family, and to figure out how to deal with family issues.

He commented that it also has helped him to bond with other people in a pro-social way. As far as I know, he is still practicing.

Students Also Share Their Ideas With Me!

Years ago, when I began the project of creating a CD for my kids, I asked them for their opinions, and worked on a script for the project. They were more than happy to share their ideas and suggestions with me.

I then put together a demo, had a group of girls from the juvenile detention center listen to it, and asked them to critique it.

Based on the comments and suggestions, a few changes were made, and it became the *InnerTeen* CD I have been giving away to my incarcerated students since the spring of 2006.

When I began writing this book, I wanted to make sure I was including all the things my students would want to see included in a book that was written at their request, and for them.

Again, I asked my students for their suggestions.

And, again, they were more than happy to share their ideas and suggestions with me. I received some wonderful feedback from my kids — four pages of notes, as a matter of fact! I have included every one of their suggestions, ideas, and requests in this book.

I doubt that I would have created my CD — or this book — had my students not requested them.

My classes, my CD, and now this book all have been created *for my students*, with major input from my students, and because my students have asked for it.

THINK TIME:

>*What knowledge do you have that you can share?*

NOTES • THOUGHTS • IDEAS:

CHAPTER THIRTY-ONE

WHAT MY STUDENTS — AND OTHERS — HAVE SHARED...

You cannot teach a man anything;
you can only help him to find it within himself.

– Galileo, scientist / astronomer

I refer to my students as "my kids" because I find myself becoming somewhat protective of them, much like a mother.

I don't concern myself with the critics of my program (there have been a few), nor anyone's opinion of my work. I only concern myself with my students.

I realize that I will not be able to reach all the kids who attend my classes, but I know with certainty that I am reaching the ones I am supposed to reach. And, I know I get through to a lot of them — they don't hesitate to let me know.

A Few Students' Comments

Over the years, I have received many comments from my students and other people — whether in class, by e-mail, or when I run into them at a store or on the street.

These students' comments — in their words — are the ones that matter the most to me, and include:

"Dear Mrs. Neal, Thank you for coming out to (juvenile detention center) on your own time. I like when you come because meditation helps me sleep at night. I like when you come out because meditation helps me get my mind off of stuff."

– (Juvenile Male)

"Mrs. Neal, I pray for you every day. You have helped me get through being locked up here at (juvenile detention center)."

— (Juvenile Male)

"You never gave up on me, but everyone else did. This has helped me deal with a lot of stuff in my life."

— (Juvenile Male)

"You are the only person I know who makes God sound cool and made me want to know how to pray. Thanks for teaching me how easy it is."

— (Juvenile Male)

"I like what you teach us at (juvenile detention center) and have practiced meditation every day. I got the CD when I left and play it for my baby, it helps her sleep too."

— (Juvenile Male)

"The kids enjoyed this class and didn't even realize how much they were learning about themselves. Very powerful class, wonderful delivery from Nancy, and oh so very beneficial to these kids."

— Youth Counselor, 2009

"What a cool way to get a message across, and actually learn something I can use in lots of areas of my life. I really liked the games and 'tests' and felt really good after the exercise. I will remember to get my CD this time when I leave."

— (Juvenile Male)

"She teaches teens positive techniques to cope with and respond to their negative feelings. Some of the boys practice her techniques outside of (her) class."

– Jessica, resident adviser, youth center

"I can't say enough about how impressed I am with Nancy's session of relaxation and meditation. At first I was pretty skeptical and suspicious about the idea because I have never experienced anything like it before. But I must admit that it felt great to clear my mind and feel the stress relief, her voice is both soothing and comforting. I literally felt my mind and thoughts become vividly clear as I sank into her amazing meditation technique. I also felt the muscles in my body relax and I felt a sort of lightness to me like weights were taken off my shoulders. Nancy has great purpose and energy which is contagious."

– Student, Peace Officer Academy Student, 2008

"Great Stuff!"

– Student, Peace Officer Academy Student, 2009

"The kids really enjoyed it and they still talk about it"

– Counselor at Local Intermediate School,
Annual "Spirit Day" Event

"I thought this was going to be so lame. Then I got out of (juvenile detention center) and realized how much I could use what you taught me. I promise I am not going to forget to get my CD this time. And I won't be back here."

– (Juvenile Female)

"Those meditation exercises you taught me helped me deal with my addiction problems. I was able to stay away from (drugs) because I thought of other stuff to do instead of doing the (drugs). It helped me to because I just relaxed when I was getting upset or angry and thought about what you told me in class."

– (Juvenile Male)

"I think it's really cool that this isn't about any religion, or anti-religion, or judgmental, but it kinda makes me think about my own spirituality."

– (Juvenile Male)

"I like how your voice is so comforting and you help us to relax. Thank you for praying for us every day like you said. I will pray for you every day, too."

– (Juvenile Male)

"Mrs. Neal! I took a breath! It worked! I didn't start a fight!"

– (Juvenile Female)

Here are a couple of letters that have touched my heart. This first one is from the sister of a juvenile who was incarcerated:

"...I would like to take the time to give a sincere thank you.

"I was on the internet looking for some tools and resources to enhance my brother's experience at the (Juvenile Rehab Center) in (city). My thought was that if I could educate myself on what the juveniles go through, that perhaps I could be a positive role model for my brother, not just someone that he could receive letters and the occasional less-than-an-hour visit from once a week.

"I wanted to do some research on things that I could write him about to help him through this time in his life. I came across a newspaper article about meditation that you offer to the juveniles.

"I just wanted to say thanks for all that you do, and all that you put into the juveniles. It really does mean a lot and I'm sure to them it's a blessing ... maybe in disguise to some of them, but I believe it's truly a blessing.

"I really believe that you're making an impact and I will definitely be writing my brother about your meditation tactics and hopefully from them, he can manage to find a moment of peace while going through his journey.

"Again, I just wanted to say thank you ... please don't stop believing in today's youth. I know first-hand how much they really need someone to just love and believe in them. I'm sure my brother and others alike would love to have you as a positive influence in their lives.

Thanks again!"
Becky

Now, last, but not least, one of my all-time favorite comments from a former student. Nicole was one of the students who participated in one of my first meditation classes.

I am particularly proud of Nicole, with whom I still keep in touch. She has worked hard to achieve her dreams, and is now helping others to achieve theirs.

"In 1995, I was only seventeen years old and filled with all of the usual teenage stress. I wasn't exactly sure where I fit in, I didn't know what I wanted to wear, and I had not yet figured out what I was going to do with myself when I grew up. I was attending the (vocational school) enrolled in the Graphic Arts program. I dreamed of becoming an art teacher after high school. Of course I was filled with the excitement of my dreams, along with the anxiety of being a teenage girl that hadn't quite figured herself out yet. I suffered from extreme anxiety wondering where and how I fit in, and wondering if I even needed to anyways.

"Then one day we had a substitute teacher in our lab. Her name was Mrs. Nancy Neal. She was the coolest adult I had ever met. She actually looked at me when she was speaking to me and she really cared about what I was interested in and why. She taught us guided meditation one day in class, and I went home and practiced on my own that very same day. I continued to do this on a regular basis. I even did it in the classroom or anywhere that I was and needed to relax. This relaxation I learned from Mrs. Neal was one of the first steps to my realization of what I wanted to spend my life doing.

"I learned from her the importance of caring for and respecting myself no matter what everyone else was saying or doing in my life. She touched the life of myself and so many

of my friends when no other adults wanted anything to do with us. My friends and I weren't put on this earth to be like everyone else and she recognized and encouraged that.

I owe her many thanks for helping me develop into an independent thinker and not be afraid to follow what sounds correct for me to live by, even if it made no sense to anyone else.

"*I am currently the owner of The Earth's Center in downtown Tipp City. I am a Holistic Health Practitioner and Holistic Life Coach. I help people learn how to relax and focus on what is important in their lives and how they can get where they want to be.*

"*I do not know how many lives Mrs. Neal has reached the way she has reached mine. I do know that my fourteen year old nephew loves her and she is one of few that can reach in and bring him out.*

"*Thank you Mrs. Neal for spending your life blessing the lives of others. What you are doing is making a difference.*"

Nicole Mikel, Owner,

The Earth's Center, Tipp City, Ohio

I am grateful that the newspaper articles about my program always have been positive and that my appearance on a local radio show was such a well-received experience. *(These are all posted at my website: www.blessingsfound.net.)*

The one thing that keeps me going more than anything else is running into a student who tells me that I made a difference in their life. There is nothing that matches that feeling — the *blessing* — I get when I encounter a student who gives me a hug and thanks me for helping them.

NOTES • THOUGHTS • IDEAS:

CHAPTER THIRTY-TWO

RANDOM COMMENTS and TIDBITS...

What happened in the past that was painful
has a great deal to do with what we are today,
but revisiting this painful past can contribute little or nothing
to what we need to do now.
– William Glasser

There is a pile of papers on my desk with lots of notes, and questions and comments from my students — including all those notes I took with information they wanted me to be sure to include in this book.

As I was looking through that pile, I realized that there were a few things I either didn't address someplace else in this book, or there just was not a logical place to address them.

So, I set aside this chapter for those things that I didn't cover adequately elsewhere...

A frequent question I hear from my students is, "How do *you* use meditation, Mrs. Neal? How does it help *you*?"

My best answer — prayer.

I always begin each day with a meditative prayer. I cannot do what I do, or keep the schedule I keep, without healthy doses of Divine Guidance!

I meditate occasionally other times during the day — especially when I am in need of a little focus or direction.

On the topic of Divine Guidance, when I feel that I am being directed by the "Big Guy" to do something — regardless of what it is — I never question it; I just do it.

My entire program — *mrs. neal's not-so-conventional meditation class for teens* — as well as my CD and this book all came into being as a result of His direction, and the encouragement and support of my students.

I spend a lot of time in my classes cautioning students about the type of music they choose to listen to, mainly because so many young people choose to listen to what I refer to as pure evil (my opinion).

A common belief is that Satan — who was one of God's favorite angels — also was the angel of music. Because I am a Christian and I believe what I read in the Bible, I believe that Satan is in a battle with God to win as any souls as he can.

It seems logical to me that Satan would pervert music and use it to corrupt young people — who can be more easily manipulated and misled. There is so much evil being spouted through the lyrics of some of the more popular music — so much hatred and violence — where else could that come from? Again, it's just my opinion, but I think it's worthy of consideration.

It's always been interesting to me that even when other areas of my life are in shambles, this program always seems to be Divinely guided, and blessed.

I realized long ago that kids needed tools that made sense to them, tools that they could use to gain some control in their lives. So, I designed my program specifically for teens, to equip them with a few healthy tools they can use — now and in their future.

—◇—

Resource for essential oils I use in class
(because students always ask):
www.spiritualskyincense.com

—◇—

To Contact Me:

I do have a website with lots of information — mostly for my students — and I encourage you to check it out. I also have no problem sharing my e-mail address with students.

Website: www.blessingsfound.net

E-mail: mrsneal@blessingsfound.net

NOTE: For those of you who have a copy of my *InnerTeen* CD (with the purple cover), ***DO NOT*** use the contact information found *inside* the CD cover— it is not monitored and will not get to me. Use ***only*** e-mail address above if you want to contact me!

I do respond to e-mails from students, usually within a few days. All I ask is that you write either "student" or "meditation" in the subject line so I don't delete your message *(I get a lot of junk mail).*

By the way, I do not text, instant message, or use any other instant social media communication. This is one of the things I choose *not* to do to keep *my* personal stress levels down.

Let me close this chapter with the following story.

While not all of my students are at-risk or incarcerated youth, quite a few of them are.

When I am asked why I volunteer so much of my time to teaching my program to these kids, I share this story — it sums up how I feel about my kids...

THE STARFISH STORY

A man and a boy were taking a walk along the beach, talking about life and sharing the beauty of the day

Along the shoreline, they came across hundreds of starfish that had washed up from the tide that were likely to die from the heat of the sun.

As they walked along, the man would pause, bend down and pick up a starfish, then toss it back into the ocean.

The boy was puzzled by this; what could the man be doing? There were so many starfish!

"I've been watching you," said the boy, "but, I don't understand. There are hundreds of starfish along this beach. You can't save all of them! Why do you waste your time? How can you possibly think that what you are doing will make a difference?"

The man smiled at the boy, bent over and picked up another starfish. As he tossed it back into the ocean, he said, "I made a difference to that one."

– This version of this story is loosely inspired by a story that is based in part on an essay, "The Star Thrower" by Loren Eiseley

NOTES • THOUGHTS • IDEAS:

NOTES • THOUGHTS • IDEAS:

RECOMMENDED READING

You cannot open a book
without learning something.
– Confucius

Students occasionally ask me to recommend books they can read to learn more about meditation, about the topics we discuss in class, or about my philosophy on life in general.

I am sure there are more books than those listed below that you would find interesting — and these represent only a fraction of my personal library — but these are just a few of *my* favorite books to get you started:

- **The Bible**

- **Healing and the Mind**
  by Bill Moyers
  Published by Doubleday, ©1993

- **The Elegant Universe**
  by Brian Greene
  Published by W.W. Norton & Co., Inc., ©1999

- **The Little Prince**
  by Antoine de Saint-Exupéry
  Published by Harcourt, Brace & World, Inc., ©1943

- **The Divine Matrix**
  by Gregg Braden
  Published by Hay House, Inc., ©2007

- *The Power of Your Subconscious Mind*
  by Joseph Murphy, Ph.D., D.D.
  Published by Reward Books/Prentiss Hall, ©2000

- *Is Your Teen Stressed or Depressed*
  by Dr. Archibald D. Hart and
  Dr. Catherine Hart Weber
  Published by Thomas Nelson, ©2005

- *Extraordinary Knowing*
  by Elizabeth Lloyd Mayer, Ph.D.
  Published by Bantam Books/Random House, ©2007

- *The Mind*
  by Richard M. Restak, M.D.
  Published by Bantam Books, ©1988

- *The Spontaneous Healing of Belief*
  by Gregg Braden
  Published by Hay House, Inc., ©2008

- *The Relaxation Response*
  by Herbert Benson, M.D.
  Published by Harper Torch/Harper Collins, ©1975

- *Coming to Our Senses: Healing Ourselves and The World Through Mindfulness*
  by Jon Kabat-Zinn
  Published by Hyperion, ©2005

- *Being in Balance*
  by Dr. Wayne W. Dyer
  Published by Hay House, ©2006

- **The Four Agreements**
  by Don Miguel Ruiz
  Published by Amber-Allene, ©1997

- **The Body has a Mind of Its Own**
  by Sandra Blakeslee and Matthew Blakeslee
  Published by Random House, ©2007

- **Getting in the Gap**
  by Dr. Wayne W. Dyer
  Published by Hay House, ©2003

- **Spontaneous Healing**
  by Andrew Weil, M.D.
  Published by Alfred A. Knopf, ©1995

- **The Isaiah Effect: Decoding the Lost Science
  of Prayer and Prophecy**
  by Gregg Braden
  Published by Three Rivers Press/Random House, ©2000

- **Breakthrough Dreaming — How to Tap the Power of Your
  24-Hour Mind**
  by Dr. Gayle Delaney
  Published by Bantam Books, ©1991

- **Our Dreaming Mind**
  by Robert L. Van de Castle, Ph.D.
  Published by Ballantine Books, a division of Random House, ©1994

NOTES • THOUGHTS • IDEAS:

FINALE — A LESSON IN EVERY CHALLENGE: ABOUT THE QUOTATIONS IN THIS BOOK...

Imagination is more important than knowledge.
For knowledge is limited to all we now know and understand,
while imagination embraces the entire world,
and all there ever will be to know and understand.

– Albert Einstein [5]

I like to think that there is a lesson in every challenge.

You may have noticed that there are a lot of quotations and stories included in this book — hopefully, you will find them as thought-provoking as I do.

I went on a journey around the world (through my computer) in order to gain permissions to use some of these inspirational treasures, and was blessed to encounter a number of wonderful people during the course of this adventure, some of whom shared additional information about a few of the quotations that I would like to share with you. *(I just can't resist turning any moment into a teaching moment!)*

Anyone who knows me knows that I have long admired Albert Einstein. You will find several of his more well-known quotations throughout this book, including the one above.

I learned a little history of those quotations which was passed along to me from Princeton University, and greatly enhanced by the Information Officer, Albert Einstein Archives, at Hebrew University of Jerusalem in Israel. I am beyond grateful for the assistance I received from Jerusalem, and this knowledge that was shared, which I now share with you!

If you take a look at the Einstein quotes in this book, you will see a little number next to his name. Following is an explanation of each of those, as explained to me:

(1) "Great spirits ..."
The complete and accurate quote was furnished to me by the Information Officer at the University of Jerusalem; frequently the last line of this quote is omitted when you see it. It is Einstein's statement on behalf of Bertrand Russell, first published in <u>New York Times</u>, March 19, 1940.

(2) "Everything is determined..."
This quote is taken from an interview* George Sylvester Viereck published in <u>The Saturday Evening Post</u> on October 26, 1929.

(3) "I want to know how God..."
Recalled by Einstein's Berlin student Esther Salaman, quoted in Salaman, "A Talk with Einstein," Listener 54 (1955).

(4) "Science without religion..."
This is from "Science, Philosophy, and Religion," Einstein's contribution to a symposium held in New York; first published by the Conference on Science, Philosophy and Religion in Their Relation to the Democratic Way of Life, NY, 1941.

(5) "Imagination is more important..."
This quote, also, is taken from the interview* George Sylvester Viereck published in <u>The Saturday Evening Post</u> in October, 1929.

*The following information also was shared with me about the Viereck interview published in The Saturday Evening Post on October 26, 1929:

> *In 1929, George Sylvester Viereck, an American journalist of German descent, interviewed Einstein in Berlin.*
>
> *Because the conversation was conducted in German, and because Viereck's was notorious for his rather casual handling of his notes — and for filling in some gaps with his own words and ideas — the reliability of the article about Einstein is undermined with various facts contained therein being identifiably doubtful or inaccurate. Therefore, it is a legitimate question whether Einstein actually said what Viereck eventually published.*
>
> *Because of this, we can neither verify nor deny it; he may have said it this way or with different words.*

I included a couple of quotations in this book that initially I had believed were Einstein's, but found out that they have been falsely attributed to Einstein; the actual author is unknown. *(The Information Officer at the Albert Einstein Archives in Jerusalem clarified this for me.)*

The quote, "Everybody is a genius. But if you judge a fish by its ability to climb a tree, it will live its whole life believing it is stupid" is one of them; it is not an authentic Einstein quote.

The other falsely attributed quote is, "There are two ways to live your life: One is as though nothing is a miracle. The other is as though everything is a miracle" which was allegedly published in 1931; however, it, too, can not be authenticated, nor can the publication. While these are wonderful quotes, they are *not* the words of Albert Einstein.

The quote *"And now here is my secret, a very simple secret..."* is an excerpt from THE LITTLE PRINCE by Antoine de Saint-Éxupery, translated from the French by Richard Howard.

Reprinted by permission (for U.S.A. and Canada) of Houghton Mifflin Harcourt Publishing Company. All rights reserved.

Copyright 1943 by Houghton Mifflin Harcourt Publishing Company. Copyright (c) renewed 1971 by Consuelo de Saint-Exupery, English translation copyright ©2000 by Richard Howard.

Permission granted to use this quotation world-wide came from Foreign Rights, Editions Gallimard, Paris, France.

The quote *"Breath is the bridge..."* is a lovely quote from a Vietnamese Zen Monk. It is from "The Miracle of Mindfulness" by Thích Nhất Hạnh. Permission was readily granted, with the request to include the following: Copyright © 1975, 1976 by Thích Nhất Hạnh; English translation Copyright © 1975, 1976, 1987 by Mobi Ho. Reprinted by permission of Beacon Press, Boston.

The Biblical scriptures found throughout this book came from my personal and very old copy of the Holy Bible — a King James version. Fortunately, the King James Holy Bible is considered to be in public domain, so copyright permission is not required.

My beloved King James version of the Holy Bible was published by The World Publishing Company, Cleveland and New York, and it was "manufactured in the United States of America."

There is no date in it, but it's an oldie. I would love to share more information about it, but that's all there is. Well, other than the many bookmarks, the lightly-yellowed pages, and the tattered edges on the cover.

In Closing...

I had wanted to include more of these inspirational tidbits, as well as more mental exercises (optical illusions, riddles, word games, etc. — such as the ones I use in class; however, permission could not be granted by the copyright holders (some were unknown and some were un-findable), and apparently, "fair use" does not apply.

May I suggest that you find books or websites with mental exercises and work out your brain on a regular basis!

And! Remember the "THINK TIME" suggestion in Chapter 28? Take time to find your own inspirational words and create your own "Inspiration Wall."

NOTES • THOUGHTS • IDEAS:

Let us be silent, that we may hear the whispers of the gods.

– Ralph Waldo Emerson, author

God bless you, kids, and remember:

You are in my prayers...

NOTES • THOUGHTS • IDEAS:

Printed in the United States
By Bookmasters